The Changing
Academic Market

NEIL J. SMELSER
ROBIN CONTENT

The Changing
Academic Market

General Trends and a
Berkeley Case Study

UNIVERSITY OF CALIFORNIA PRESS

BERKELEY LOS ANGELES LONDON

University of California Press
Berkeley and Los Angeles, California
University of California Press, Ltd.
London, England
© 1980 by
The Regents of the University of California
ISBN 0-520-03753-7
Library of Congress Catalog Card Number: 78-62840
Printed in the United States of America

1 2 3 4 5 6 7 8 9

Contents

Preface

This book concerns the changing academic market in the 1970s. Unlike most treatments of the subject, however, it will scan that market at both macroscopic and microscopic levels. Because of this unusual combination, we should say something, before we begin, about the circumstances in which the book developed, our rationale for writing it, and how we have organized it.

In the summer of 1975 Smelser was beginning the second year of an assignment as Chairman of the Department of Sociology at the University of California, Berkeley, and Content was beginning her third year as Assistant to the Chairman, a position which involved supervision of the non-academic staff in the Department (about eight in number) and coordinating most of the Department's administrative business. Their two positions together constituted the center of the Department's administration.

The Department, after having experienced an extraordinary growth of faculty in the 1950s and early 1960s, had gradually settled into a "steady state" in the late 1960s and early 1970s, averaging approximately one appointment each year after 1971, usually to replace some other faculty member who had retired, resigned or failed to gain promotion to tenure. That settling process reflected in microcosm the general "no-growth" situation in the University of California at

Berkeley, and also reflected the dramatic tightening of demand for academics in general and sociologists in particular in the early 1970s. We had been made aware of this altered market situation not only by the restrictions on our new appointments, but by the increasing difficulty in placing our graduate students at other institutions as they were completing their doctorates.

The new market situation had not changed by the summer of 1975. By a series of circumstances, however, the Department suddenly found itself with the promise of five or six new vacancies over a period of two years, caused by the coincidental occurrence of two retirements, two non-promotions, and one resignation. The Berkeley administration granted the department permission to make three (ultimately, four) new appointments in the academic year 1975–76.

To appoint several new faculty members constituted at once a welcome opportunity and a matter of serious concern to us. The opportunity was straightforwardly one of being able to build departmental resources substantially for the future after a prolonged famine. The concerns were many. We knew that the work involved in processing the flood of applicants for several positions was going to be phenomenal; we knew how limited our own resources were for completing that work; we knew that we were already in an era of "affirmative action," which imposed a number of complex procedures to be observed in any search-and-appointment process; and we were aware of a number of divisions and conflicts in the Department, which often ran so deep as to make it difficult for the faculty to arrive at consensus on any decision, including a decision to offer positions to specific candidates.

During the year that followed we designed a recruitment plan; secured the cooperation of numerous constituencies in supporting and carrying out that plan; carried to completion the evaluation of nearly 300 candidates who applied for the positions; secured a reasonable if sometimes precarious faculty consensus on several leading candidates; and ultimately filled the positions with the candidates of the Department's choice. The story of that search constitutes a substantial portion of this volume.

An initial set of questions might occur to the reader: Why bother to document the search? What can be learned from a single search and appointment process in a single department in a single year? These questions occurred to us early, and we would like to voice several reasons why we believe our report might have some general interest and be of some general value.

First, we reveal in this volume a kind of information that is seldom made public. Academic departments do write down a great deal of information on great amounts of paper, but the business of department meetings—to say nothing of informal interaction in the corridors—is seldom recorded in written form. We hope to record a certain amount of information of this type, hopefully within the bounds of discretion. Beyond this, we conducted our search in a sufficiently systematic way that large amounts of comparable data on each of our candidates was recorded in the process. This kind of recording is also unusual in recruitment processes in higher education, which in many quarters retain their informal, word-of-mouth character. This abundance of information provided an opportunity to analyze the origins and characteristics of our pool of candidates, and to throw some light on prevailing knowledge, assumptions, and myths about processes in the academic labor market.

Second, we feel it important to communicate the results of our work to others who are attempting to fashion their own solutions in the contemporary market. During the course of our research we had occasion to talk with dozens of others in the "recruitment business" who were attempting to meet the exigencies imposed by the buyer's market, by affirmative action, and by the generally uncertain situation in higher education. It is our impression that, consistent with the tradition of decentralization in American higher education, everybody is inventing the wheel anew, that there is little interchange of information on problem-solving, and that there is little effort on the part of institutions of higher education to learn from the successes and failures of other institutions. We believe that to report our experience will work modestly toward increasing the flow of information.

Third, we have an interest in candidates, present and future. In many respects they are the most evident victims of the current crisis in the academic market, since they are the ones who apply more or less "cold" to many institutions, who are kept waiting without word for sometimes as long as months, and who are disappointed after that wait. In our own search we came to appreciate how little information is imparted to candidates, how high their anxieties are, and how much brutalization they undergo in striving for positions. Much of this is inevitable, given present market conditions, but we believe that a report of the recruitment process from the point of view of those "on the other side" might provide some information and insight for candidates.

Fourth—and most important in our own mnds—scholars and analysts seldom attempt to examine the interplay of large economic, political, and social forces now buffetting higher education in America at microcosmic levels—that is to say, at the level of the single organization and at the level of the individual human being. Those great forces are not "above" us; they impinge on our purposive daily activity and continuously have to be taken into account. We hope to communicate in some degree how that process works, and how we attempt to manage in an increasingly uncertain institutional environment.

Chapter One is a general analysis of academic recruitment in its market context, in which we argue that it is less "economic" than other markets because many values other than economic ones operate as determinants of market behavior, and it is subject to restraints on mobility and lack of information. We also identify a number of political and ideological dimensions involved in the recruitment of academic personnel.

Chapter Two concerns market dynamics. We trace the implications of some of the peculiarities identified in Chapter One, plus a few additional ones, for fluctuations in supply and demand. We note that the academic market is subject to extreme swings and to rigidity in the ability of supply to adjust to changing demand conditions, and we provide some empirical evidence of the supply-demand dynamics during the past two decades, both for the American academic market in general and for sociology in particular.

Chapter Three presents some evidence of the ways in which academic departments and other agencies have responded to the new, tighter market conditions. Our account is based on evidence gathered while visiting a number of sister institutions and interviewing individuals about their recruitment and placement policies and procedures. We conclude that the sociologists' response has been somewhat sluggish, that old procedures and methods persist, that adaptations are minimal and incremental, and that very few institutions appear to be learning from what other institutions are doing or not doing to adapt to a radically different personnel situation.

With this general background, we turn to our own story, which begins with a bit of department history in Chapter Four, tracing the Department's vicissitudes of growth and non-growth and some of the personnel procedures on which it has relied in the past. More particularly, we give a brief account of an unsuccessful personnel search conducted in the academic year 1974–75, a search which disappointed us, informed us of some of the current realities of the academic market, and instructed us of the necessity to change our ways in the coming year.

Chapter Five describes how our opportunity for a really ambitious search arose, as well as the early negotiations with

the campus administration regarding that search. We also record our early thinking, especially the very extensive plans
we made to generate an exhaustive and equitable search.

In Chapter Six we discuss how the plan we had generated
unfolded in reality. We conclude that the search was a successful one, but one that was forever threatening to founder
through lack of support, practical failures, lack of communication and miscommunication, and political conflict.

In Chapter Seven the characteristics of our candidates are
described. We look at their institutional origins—that is,
their Ph.D.-granting university—as well as the sources from
which we learned about their candidacy. We show how many
minorities and women were considered, where their applications originated, and how well they fared comparatively in
competition for the several positions.

Finally, in Chapter Eight we draw a few lessons from our
analysis and venture a few recommendations for others em-
barking on enterprises similar to ours.

In writing this account we have been as objective as we
could, given our role as participants. We have also deliberately not concealed anything that might be regarded by some
as Departmental "dirty linen," though we have stopped short
of including material that might be regarded as damaging to
any individual. Therefore we have chosen either to disguise or
not to reveal the names of anyone other than ourselves,
though we realize that it would be easy, with a little detective
work, to identify some of the persons involved in the search.
We have asked many of those involved, either as candidates
or as recruiters, to read the manuscript and advise us on its ac-
curacy, appropriateness, and tactfulness. We responded as
best we could to their reactions before preparing the final version of the manuscript.

We realize that in making everyone but ourselves anonymous, we risk creating the impression that we were the principal managers of the show, and that everyone else was
lurking unimportantly in the background. Nothing could be
further from the truth. The faculty was heavily and responsi-

bly involved in the evaluation and selection process, as were a number of graduate students in the Department. The Berkeley administration independently authorized and oversaw the operation with a basically supportive attitude. And those candidates who were called upon to make decisions in response to our offers did so on their own. As our account will show, it was far from a "controlled" operation.

We should like to thank Betty Lou Bradshaw, whose research assistance was invaluable, and Christine Egan, who flawlessly coordinated communication between those of us working on the project and efficiently processed the manuscript at various stages of its development. We should also like to thank those several anonymous readers who were participants in the search for evaluating our material. Last but not least, we extend thanks to the Ford Foundation, which provided a grant to cover research costs, and especially to Peter de Janosi of its Higher Education Division for his support of the project.

N.J.S. and R.C.

CHAPTER 1

General Contours of an Academic Market

The market for academic services is something of a nightmare for economists. It is a honeycomb of ignorance, of economically "irrational" behavior, and of obstacles to mobility of resources. After a comprehensive study of market structure and patterns of mobility, the economist David Brown concluded somewhat mournfully that the academic market was a "maverick," and ventured a number of recommendations that would bring its structure and functioning closer to that of a competitive economic market.[1] What are its imperfections, and what consequences do they have for market processes?

INGREDIENTS OF CLASSICAL WAGE THEORY

In the classical labor market, the firm is prepared to offer wages at a level in accord with the marginal value that the labor at a given level of skill will bring to the productive process. On the side of the laborer, he is willing to offer labor in given amounts, depending on the level of disutility that the labor involves and the level of monetary rewards offered. On each side of the market, the conditions of offer are thus informed by a kind of utility function—or economic rationality, if you will—which governs the

---

1. David G. Brown, *The Mobile Professors* (Washington, D.C.: American Council of Education, 1967), p. 61.

terms of exchange. That exchange takes place, moreover, at an equilibrium point where the demand and supply functions intersect. In such a market, moreover, it is assumed that the primary sanctions are monetary rewards, that resources are more or less completely mobile, that both buyers and sellers have complete information about market conditions, and that neither buyer nor seller has the power to influence the aggregate output of services or the wage level at which they are exchanged.[2] On every count, the market for academic services complicates these assumptions, and in many cases deviates so far from them as to render them virtually invalid.

THE NATURE OF THE SELLERS AND BUYERS

By "market for academic services," we refer to that area where institutions of higher education secure the services of persons who teach and perform related activities in those institutions. The "buyers" are the hiring institutions, and the "sellers" are individuals who have received graduate training in some academic field in an institution of higher education.

Immediately it must be noted that we have defined not a single market but a multiplicity of overlapping markets. Among the buyers, large research and graduate-training institutions are in the market for a different kind of service than are institutions which specialize in undergraduate teaching alone, and institutions which offer only two years of college teaching look for yet another range of skills in their prospective employees. These institutions could be subdivided even further according to whether they are large or small, public or private, secular or religious, and so on. There is also diversity on the supply side. We must distinguish, at the very least, between a market for people who will do research and train graduate students, and a

2. For a more detailed statement of these ingredients, see *ibid.,* pp. 48–60.

market for people who will teach at the undergraduate level alone; these two markets overlap but are in some respects separate from one another.

In this chapter we concentrate mainly on the market for people with skills or promise in the area of research and graduate training, since that is the setting for our own case study. What are the distinctive characteristics of their services? First, these services have a long gestation period. Putting to one side the years of study that must precede entry into Ph.D. training programs, completing those programs requires from three to more than ten years.[3] Furthermore, the labor force—that is, the pool of Ph.D.'s—is highly differentiated by quality and extent of training, special fields of competence and interest, and relative emphasis on research and teaching. So divided and sub-divided has the market for Ph.D.'s become, Brown concluded, that its units lack interchangeability. This reduces the effective level of competition among Ph.D.'s.[4] Certainly it is rare for one academic discipline to hire outside its own ranks, and each discipline is divided into numerous groups of subspecialists who tend to hire their own but not other specialists (for example, econometricians hire econometricians, economic historians hire economic historians, and so on).

The market for academic services is further complicated by variations in the extent to which holders of advanced degrees are hired in the academic and non-academic sectors. The proportion of chemistry Ph.D.'s hired in industry and other non-academic sectors, for example, is much higher than the proportion in anthropology. Within the social sciences, Cartter calculated—on the basis of 1974 figures—that the percentage of anthropologists finding

3. According to Cartter's calculations, the average required time taken to complete a Ph.D. from entry to completion is six years; elapsed time from baccalaureate to doctorate averages 8.2 years. Allan M. Cartter, *Ph.D.'s and the Academic Labor Market* (New York: McGraw-Hill, 1972), pp. 1–2.

4. Brown, *The Mobile Professors,* pp. 56–60.

employment in academic institutions is 86.0; for political science 77.7; for economics 70.1; and for psychology 54.0[5] For sociology, approximately 75 percent of doctorates have found employment in universities and colleges over the past several decades.[6]

ACADEMIC VALUES AND THE UTILITY FUNCTION OF ACADEMICS

One of the facts that struck Brown in his study of faculty mobility in the 1960s is that professors did not respond consistently to different salary levels. "To a considerable extent, professors fail to accept the offers from the institutions that would pay them the highest salary and place them at the highest rank."[7] He concluded from this that "many of the laborers in the groves of academe are not economic men and this gives rise to a market imperfection."[8] If academics, then, are only partially economic men, what are their values, and what kinds of rewards do they seek?

Focusing still on that sector of the academic market that involves research and graduate training, we submit that the dominant institutionalized value in this sector can be described by the term "excellence in science and scholarship."[9] Invoking such a value means evaluating academics' performance in accord with accepted canons of logical adequacy and empirical validity of knowledge produced, as well as canons of "creativity," or the generation of new knowledge and insights. Those who conform best to these

5. Cartter, *Ph.D.'s and the Academic Labor Market*, p. 225.
6. Sharon K. Panian and Melvin L. DeFleur, *Sociologists in Non-Academic Employment* (Washington, D.C.: American Sociological Association, 1976), pp. 3, 47.
7. Brown, *The Mobile Professors*, p. 58.
8. Ibid.
9. This value is closely related to what Parsons and Platt refer to as "cognitive rationality." Talcott Parsons and Gerald Platt, *The American University* (Cambridge: Harvard University Press, 1973).

canons are regarded as the most worthy. The criteria for excellence differ, of course, from discipline to discipline. Canons of excellence in mathematics focus on the extent to which work is logically adequate, novel, and "elegant." In the physical sciences many of the same canons apply, with additional criteria of empirical adequacy, as measured by guidelines of research. The social sciences also stress theoretical and empirical excellence, although the guidelines for excellent research in these disciplines differ from those in the natural sciences. (Typically, too, the criteria for excellence in the social sciences are not often as clear and agreed-upon as those in the natural sciences.) Assessment of historical research invokes canons of painstaking and thorough scholarship, attention to the authenticity of historical data, and imagination in reconstructing historical processes in the most consistent or plausible ways. Finally, many studies in the humanities, such as literary analysis, are valued most for extracting the most consistent, original, and "rich" meaning from cultural products. Despite these different emphases in the application of the criteria of excellence, such criteria are the primary ones used in the evaluation of academics and their work.

What are the normative expectations regarding motivation, recruitment, training, and rewards that usually accompany this value of excellence in science and scholarship? Typically it is expected that the principal motivational component in the makeup of an academic is a sense of dedication that will act as a spur to a relentless, scrupulous, even obsessional pursuit of cognitively valid knowledge.[10] With respect to recruitment for research roles, the principle of universalistic achievement in relation to the criteria of excellence has been institutionalized in extreme

---

10. This expectation is close to—and, indeed, probably historically derived from—what Weber termed a religious "calling." Max Weber, *The Protestant Ethic and the Spirit of Capitalism,* trans. Talcott Parsons (New York: Charles Scribner's Sons, 1958).

form, with elaborate (though not always successful) efforts to exclude criteria such as kinship ties, political affiliation, religious denomination, and personal attractiveness as bases for such recruitment. In addition to attempting to secure the most dedicated and talented personnel, the research enterprise has institutionalized a prolonged period of apprenticeship for those who enter that enterprise, involving years of tutelage by accomplished senior research personnel, along with increasingly responsible involvement in the research enterprise itself. Finally—as if motivation, ability, socialization, and training were not enough—academic research has a complex system of rewards whereby those who succeed are catapulted to heights of prestige, esteem, and honor, leaving the less successful behind to admire them and emulate their accomplishments. Most of the features of the research enterprise, in short, can be understood as means to recruit, train, and reward the creative few.

What are the implications of these institutionalized values and normative expectations for economic supply and demand? The market for services of those in academic research is one in which the *primary* reward is not monetary compensation; it is, rather, prestige. Monetary rewards accompanying academic performance are better regarded as a kind of "floor" which will provide a base for a reasonably secure and comfortable existence, and also as an appropriate symbolic reflection of the prestige or esteem of the creative academic. This implies that monetary rewards should be regarded not as inducements proffered to secure specific performances, but rather as symbolic recognition of past, current, or promised performances. If the allocation of academic services is to be characterized in market terms, then surely the principal operative currency is prestige.

If academics are inclined mainly to seek honor and prestige, it is equally true that those are the rewards that the academy has to offer. Universities themselves are ranked—with varying degrees of exactitude—according to prestige, and being a faculty member at one rather than another becomes a tangible component of that complex of factors symbolizing prestige. Universities also have numerous institutional arrangements and symbols that underscore the inequalities of prestige of academics, such as academic ranks, awards, citations, honorary research lectures, and honorary degrees. Complementing these are signs of honor and prestige afforded by professional associations, learned societies, and other organizations, such as awards and prizes, election to membership, appointment to boards of directors of foundations, or selection for service on important government task forces.

Finally, the universities also attempt to maximize their own prestige. This is accomplished mainly by securing the best research and graduate training personnel that are available. Competition for academic talent, then, is simultaneously a competition *for* individual services and a competition *between* universities trying to advance or solidify their own position in the prestige hierarchy.

Over time, such competition for prestigious personnel has evolved into a system of extreme inequality of prestige among institutions, with a concentration of talent and prestige in a relatively few. This pattern of inequality, moreover, is self-sustaining. Because the principal currency in the market for academic research personnel is prestige, those institutions that are the most prestigious have, by that circumstance, more prestige to offer to those regarded as the most gifted, accomplished, and promising academics. Securing the services of those academics, moreover, contributes further to the prestige of those institutions. Universal in its search for talent, the research and graduate-training enterprise emerges as a very elitist complex, with its ultimate concentration of talents and rewards.

The emerging recruitment pattern is that the relatively few institutions at the top of the prestige hierarchy recruit from one another but not from below, while those lower in

the hierarchy recruit from above and laterally. Classifying
institutions of higher education into five prestige levels,
and basing that classification on various surveys of
academics, Cartter summarized the placement of recipients
of doctorates as follows:

In 1968 the top ten universities hired 69 percent of their new
doctorates from universities within the top ten, and did not
draw significantly from universities in groups 3–5. The next 20
universities hired 52 percent of their new doctorate faculty from
within their own group, 27 percent from group 1, and only 16
percent from group 3. Only in groups 4 and 5 is there a
tendency to draw the majority of faculty from superior
universities.

The most elite four-year colleges draw almost entirely from
group 1 and 2 universities, while lower-prestige colleges increasingly draw from lower-rank universities. Community colleges
and secondary school Ph.D.'s come from primarily middle-
ranked universities.[11]

For sociology, in particular, the pattern is similar. Studying the composition of the top twenty departments for the
nation—ranked, again, on the basis of faculty surveys—
Gross found that as of 1965, 86 percent of those teaching
at the graduate level in those departments were hired from
within the list of twenty. Furthermore, 73 percent of the
faculty in the top five departments received their degrees
from either their own department or another of the five;
and 48 percent of the Ph.D. faculty teaching in the top
twenty departments received their degrees from the top
five departments. Moreover, since the top institutions produce a relatively large proportion of total Ph.D.'s—the top
five produced nearly one-third of all degrees granted in
sociology—the general market process involves a "trick-
ling down" of persons *trained* at elite institutions to *employment* in institutions of lesser prestige. Only 10 percent
of the graduates at the top twenty institutions between

11. Cartter, *Ph.D.'s and the Academic Labor Market,* pp. 198–199.

1920 and 1961 had found placement in the graduate faculties of the top twenty as of 1965.[12]

MORE VARIATIONS AND IDIOSYNCRACIES

We have focused primarily so far on a few fundamental differences between a perfectly competitive economic market, classically conceived, and the market for talent in academic research and graduate training. Now we shall note four additional peculiarities that the academic market manifests: (1) institutional sources of inflexibility and immobility; (2) variations in consensus on the criteria by which excellence and promise are assessed; (3) variations in levels of information, or ignorance, in the market; (4) variations in the degree to which criteria that are alternative to—and possibly competitive with or contradictory to—universal criteria of excellence enter into the recruitment process.

1. *Institutional Sources of Inflexibility and Immobility*

Free mobility of resources—in this case, faculty members—in response to economic demands is inhibited by a number of institutional arrangements regulating their employment. Foremost among these is the institution of tenure and practices related to it. The typical career pattern is that a young academic is appointed to a junior position—instructor or assistant professor—for a probationary period of time, perhaps five to seven years. Formally, employment contracts during this period are renewed annually, and academic reviews of the faculty member occur periodically; rarely, however, is a faculty member relieved of his or her position before the probationary period is over and a decision on tenure is made. If that de-

12. George R. Gross, "The Organization Set: A Study of Sociology Departments," *The American Sociologist,* Vol. 5 (1970), pp. 25–29. For similar findings, see Davis Shichor, "Prestige of Sociology Departments and the Placing of New Ph.D.'s," *The American Sociologist,* Vol. 5 (1970), pp. 157–160.

cision is favorable, the faculty member is granted security of tenure, which implies—actually if not formally, since contracts may continue to be renewed on an annual basis—permanent employment until retirement. Such a career pattern does not inhibit mobility altogether; indeed, if a faculty member is not awarded tenure in a given institution, he or she is *forced* to move elsewhere; and, particularly under brisk market conditions, tenured faculty members may be lured to other institutions to accept more attractive positions.[13] Nevertheless, tenure gives a faculty member an exceptionally strong claim on his or her position. Morever, such an arrangement is far removed from one of Weber's conditions for "formally free labor" —namely, that workers should not appropriate jobs.[14]

The rate of mobility is also inhibited by the fact that salaries are paid on an annual basis, and movement from one institution to another takes place only on a once-a-year basis. Add to this the fact that various conventions prohibit institutions from "raiding" faculty from others after a certain date in the calendar year, and that sometimes institutions within the same region or system develop "gentlemen's agreements" restricting recruitment from one another's faculties. And in the longer run, the more time a faculty member remains in one institution, the more he or she becomes locked into its system of fringe benefits— particularly its retirement system—and the more costly it becomes to move elsewhere. A final inhibitor is the intangible but real sentiment among faculty that a person who shifts academic positions "too often" is likely to be regarded as some kind of academic entrepreneur or

13. In Brown's study, conducted in 1965 when the market for academics was clearly a seller's market, over one-fourth of those faculty members switching positions left tenured positions. *The Mobile Professors,* p. 52.

14. Max Weber, *Economy and Society: An Outline of Interpretive Sociology,* edited by Guenther Roth and Claus Wittich (New York: Bedminister Press, 1968), I, 162.

operator.[15] All these factors conspire to make the market for talent in academic research and graduate training relatively sluggish in responding to salary differentials and other economic incentives.

2. *Variations in Consensus on the Criteria by Which Excellence and Promise are Assessed*

The levels of certainty about and consensus on the criteria of "excellence in science and scholarship" used to hire academic researchers and graduate-training personnel are variable; this complicates the recruitment process, and permits or even encourages the intrusion of criteria other than decisively demonstrated excellence or promise.

The variability in recruitment criteria exists because academic disciplines differ greatly in the degree to which their practitioners agree on the acceptability or legitimacy of the discipline's basic theories and methodologies, as well as the degree to which excellent and creative performance can be assessed within them. Indeed, it is possible to envision a rough continuum with exactitude and consensus on one end and inexactitude and lack of consensus on the other. At the former would be "hard" sciences such as astronomy and physics, as well as mathematics and formal logic; at the other would be certain subjects in the humanities, such as literary or musical criticism. The various social and behavioral sciences occupy some intermediary position, with economics and some branches of physiological and learning psychology approaching the life and natural sciences more, and other subjects, such as political science and sociology, leaning more toward the humanities.

Sociology in particular has an internal variability among its own sub-fields, so that subjects such as demography and social stratification have greater paradigmatic coherence and consensus than deviance, criminology, sociology of the

15. Brown, *The Mobile Professors,* pp. 50–53.

family, and some parts of social psychology. Other paradigmatic divisions characterize the field also, as the labels of its dominant theoretical "schools" suggest— functionalism, conflict sociology, structuralism, exchange theory, and symbolic interactionism. These approaches involve differences in initial assumptions, problems posed, research methods, and explanatory modes. Though there is widespread commitment to the notion that sociology should strive to become a "science" with scientifically valid knowledge, there are a number of different models of what kind of science that should be, as well as a number of different methodologies that are believed to constitute the preferred road to scientific status.[16]

Given this diversity of paradigmatic and methodological bases, it is manifestly difficult if not impossible to combine the assessments that might be made on all these bases into a single, decisive, and unambiguous scale on which sociologists could be ranked in terms of their excellence in science and scholarship. There are, rather, numerous criteria having varying degrees of precision, and, depending on which different set of criteria is invoked, corresponding differences in evaluation appear. To translate this general point into the vocabulary of the market, the level of paradigmatic and methodological consensus is such that precise, unambiguous information about the product is not available.

3. *Variations in Levels of Ignorance in the Market*

Beyond an inevitable level of uncertainty imposed by the diversity of criteria just described, the academic market is typically characterized by a condition of buyers' limited information about the pool of potential recruits and recruits' limited information about job opportunities. In Brown's 1965 survey of academic recruits, 35 percent of the newly hired professors rated opportunities for finding jobs in their field as either "poor" or "very poor." As for

16. For an effort to estimate the kinds of divisions that characterized the Berkeley sociology faculty in the early 1970s, see Chapter Five.

employers, "for most positions, no more than four or five candidates are considered seriously, and except for the beginning positions, employers rarely recognize more than ten potential suppliers."[17] It should be kept in mind, however, that Brown's survey was completed at a time when the market was brisk. Changes in market conditions since that time have increased information about market conditions; sellers have become more aggressive in seeking opportunities, buyers have come to advertise their openings more widely, and the entire recruitment process has become increasingly preoccupied with procedural matters.

The academic market, though imperfect as a type because of lack of information, continues to operate as such: decisions about recruitment and decisions to accept places are still made, even in the face of uncertainty and ignorance. On what grounds, then, are such decisions made? In general, when individuals and organizations lack both complete information and ways to secure such information, they tend to fill in the gap with some new, usually simplified form of "knowledge"—a myth, a stereotype, a rule of thumb, "common sense," or perhaps some magical belief. Or, alternatively, they may rely on the judgment of some authority or other person whom they believe might have superior information. Or, they may rely on the results of some kind of political process in which an agreement on a line of action is generated by forming a consensus from an initially diverse set of definitions and evaluations of a situation. We should expect, then, under conditions of limited information, some alternative criteria or mechanisms for decision-making to arise, and if those conditions are more or less chronic, we should expect those criteria and mechanisms to persist.

"Networks of influence" among professional academic colleagues are often believed to be among the most important mechanisms for allocating talent for research and graduate training in the academy. One of the most forceful statements of the power of networks in the market is the

17. Brown, *The Mobile Professors*, p. 56.

case made in 1958 by Theodore Caplow and Reece McGee in *The Academic Marketplace*.[18] Although their account may be somewhat caricatured in places and, when accurate, applicable mainly to a rapidly expanding seller's market, it is nevertheless helpful in fathoming the dynamic interplay between information, prestige, and influence in the academic market, and in providing a base line for anticipating the changes in that interplay that might be expected when the market moves in the direction of a buyer's market.

Caplow and McGee were interested in describing, accounting for, and evaluating the effectiveness of existing methods of discovering and assessing academic candidates; accounting for the facts that determine an academic institution's attractiveness to candidates; and discovering the criteria actually used in faculty hiring and promotion. Their units of study were some 237 vacancies-and-replacements that occurred in nine major research universities—major in terms of numbers of Ph.D.'s granted, though variable in prestige, region, and public-private status—during the academic years 1954–55 and 1955–56. The main source of data was open-ended interview questions posed to chairmen and other faculty members of the departments with vacancies. The authors remarked on the context of expansion in which their study was conducted:

Since 1945, universities have grown at an unprecedented rate, with little structural reorganization, and little improvement of educational or administrative procedures. The growth of the past decade will probably be far surpassed in the next few years. The combined effect of a sharp rise in the adolescent population and a steady increase in the tendency to seek higher education will send enrollments soaring.[19]

In their particular sample, Caplow and McGee found "resignation" as the principal reason for vacancies occurring; resignation, moreover, usually meant simultaneously

18. New York: Basic Books, 1958.   19. Ibid., p. 41.

accepting an appointment in another institution. This phenomenon is consistent with our expectations about what occurs with high demand in a market in which producers of Ph.D.'s cannot meet that demand in the short run: institutions, striving to meet their own expanding needs, will attempt not only to discover new talent but also to attract known talent from other institutions.

Of the many facets of the academic marketplace touched by Caplow and McGee, three in particular interest us: the availability of information in the recruitment process; the role of networks of influence in that process; and the role of differential individual and institutional prestige in that process.

Under the heading of "information," Caplow and McGee based their discussion on a distinction between two kinds of recruitment—open or competitive hiring, and closed or preferential hiring. In the model situation of open recruiting:

> The department seeking a replacement attempts to procure the services of an ideal academic man. Regardless of the rank at which he is to be hired, he must be young. He must have shown considerable research productivity, or the promise of being able to produce research. He must be a capable teacher with a pleasing personality which will offend neither students, deans, nor colleagues. In order to secure the very best man available, the department simultaneously announces the opening in many quarters and obtains a long list of candidates named by their sponsors. When a sufficient number of high-caliber candidates have applied for the position, the department members shift and weight the qualifications of each most carefully in order to identify the one who best meets their requirements. This is the model hiring situation.[20]

20. Ibid., pp. 109–110. In this quotation, as well as throughout *The Academic Marketplace*, candidates are referred to simply as "men." This alone gives evidence of a significant change that has occurred between 1958 and the present, in which such usage is effectively taboo. In only a few places do Caplow and McGee mention women: "women tend to be discriminated against because they are outside the prestige system entirely and for this reason are of no use to a department in future recruitment" (p. 111). This point is repeated on p. 226.

What gives this process its "model" character? First, it involves a thorough public search; second, it involves every effort to maximize information about candidates in the decision-making process; and, finally, it stresses universalistic criteria of excellence and promise in research and teaching.[21] (The "model" character of the process is flawed, perhaps, by reference to the candidate's "pleasing personality," which suggests the intrusion of a criterion other than those of excellence and promise.)

According to Caplow and McGee, however, this ideal situation holds only "in a small percentage of cases." In most instances, "the outlines are blurred and distorted by a host of other factors."[22] Foremost among these was a deficiency of information—the absence of publicity of vacancies and the absence of a serious search for candidates. In many cases, judging from the authors' data, when a vacancy appeared, someone was approached and asked to fill it. In their sample, 52 percent of the assistant professors and 61 percent of the associate professors were reported not to have applied for vacancies; rather, they appear to have been recommended, then contacted.[23] Sometimes, the authors stated, there was a ceremonial canvassing for a roster of candidates, in the form of seeking nominations; but this was only carried out when time allowed; in general, "men are hired where they are found."[24] When contact was made between a potential hiring department and potential candidate, the information flow was also imperfect, because department chairmen had an interest in covering up any negative features of their own department (such as departmental feuds), and the candidate had an interest in covering any flaws he might have.[25] The evaluation process itself was characterized by a sloppiness and inattention to information; "it is not an overgeneralization," Caplow and

21. In stressing these latter criteria, Caplow and McGee are affirming our earlier assertion concerning the central place of "excellence" as a value for legitimizing the distribution of rewards in the academy.

22. *The Academic Marketplace*, p. 110.   23. Ibid., p. 111.

24. Ibid., p. 131.   25. Ibid, pp. 106–7.

McGee stated, "to say that departments do not, as a rule, consider teaching, academic records, or theses."[26] And finally, once a personnel decision was made, the reasons for that decision were often obscure. Chairmen would discuss the appointee's qualifications, but would rarely reveal to the administration the procedures by which he was selected; Caplow and McGee also noted many complaints from faculty members that "they were never told exactly why a given colleague was hired or fired or what he had or did not have that someone else had or did not have."[27]

If information appears to have played such a small and problematic role in the recruitment process, what factors were important? Or, to refer to our earlier questions, what kind of alternative, shorthand basis for decision-making served as a substitute? On this issue Caplow and McGee pointed directly to processes of *personal influence among networks of colleagues.* They repeatedly uncovered situations in which some candidate was given preferential consideration because of a personal relationship between members of the hiring department and colleagues elsewhere. The most frequently given reason for hiring a candidate was "he knew someone here."[28] For younger candidates, hiring departments relied almost exclusively on the recommendations of established scholars who were sponsoring them.

In places, Caplow and McGee argued, in effect, that reliance on information and reliance on personal influence in recruitment were negatively related to one another. Summarizing the function of placement bureaus at professional meetings and conventions (which are in fact central places for providing, receiving, and processing information), they said that "prestige is attached to the non-use of their services."[29] Elaborating on that statement, they argued that, being public and non-selective with respect to

26. Ibid., p. 127. We regard this statement as one of the more flagrant of the overgeneralizations to be found in the Caplow and McGee report.
27. Ibid., p. 61.   28. Ibid., p. 110.   29. Ibid., p. 120.

applicants, these placement services have no way of guaranteeing the quality or the academic respectability of a candidate in the way that a letter of reference from a known and influential colleague can. Departments, interested in safeguarding themselves against "ridiculous choices" that could damage their reputation, did so by relying on known and trusted sources.[30]

Personal contact and influence alone, however, yielded only a partial account of how the recruitment system worked. The worthiness of a candidate could not be guaranteed by a letter of recommendation from just any sponsor from just any institution. It had to come from someone who was "known" and who "counted." The flow of contact and influence was differential, and depended above all on the *prestige* of the individual and the institution from which it emanated. Prestige, for Caplow and McGee, is a kind of ephemeral quality—"not a direct measure of productivity but a composite of subjective opinion"—with which sponsors endow their students.[31] This quality subsequently determines their placement:

> There is . . . a tendency for new Ph.D.'s to enter the market in a cohort, with a distribution of prestige roughly proportional to that of their sponsors. Those new men from the most prestigeful departments with the most prestigeful sponsors will be distributed to the vacancies in departments of high prestige; the group on the next lower prestige level will probably seek and find positions in departments with slightly lower prestige, and so forth. Thus, departments at every prestige level tend to be supplied with recruits whose potential prestige level matches that of their own members.[32]

Such a formulation brings to mind our earlier observation that prestige is the major currency of the academic marketplace. As Caplow and McGee saw it, the whole market process could be regarded as a continuous effort on the part

30. Ibid., p. 121.   31. Ibid., p. 128.   32. Ibid., p. 168.

of institutions to secure the most prestigious individuals
and of individuals to seek appointments in the most prestigious institutions. Prestige, moreover, seemed more
powerful than other currencies. Institutions were willing
to go to various lengths, such as reducing teaching loads,
to secure the most promising and prestigious candidates.
Furthermore, if an institution had a low level of prestige,
it had to pay more in salary to attract candidates; Caplow
and McGee pointed out that if an individual went to an institution of lower prestige, he was usually rewarded with a
higher rank or salary than that of the institution from
which he was coming, and vice versa.[33]

Of what does prestige consist, according to Caplow and
McGee's estimation? For the individual, it consists of subjective opinions about how excellent his or her future
might be. "The academic labor market is an exchange
where universities speculate in future prestige values, based
on yet undone research."[34] Because prestige is subjective,
"consisting, in essence, of what other people think about a
man," there are "no objective means by which future
prestige can be measured."[35] Caplow and McGee explained
several features of the recruitment process by referring to
the subjectivity of judgments about prestige. The first
feature is the great elaboration of complex and time-
consuming procedures in that process. Since prestige cannot be measured in any objective way, these procedures
operate as a means of reducing "anxieties attendant upon
the comparison of candidates by estimation of their disciplinary prestige."[36] Such procedures also provide a mechanism for achieving "consensus at any price" in a world in
which there is no real basis for consensus.[37] The second is
recruiters' inattention to candidates' credentials: "[there] is
very little point in trying to determine how good the man
really is, or even how good the department opinion of him
may be. What is important is what others in the discipline

33. Ibid., pp. 147–49.   34. Ibid., p. 122.   35. Ibid., p. 122.
36. Ibid., p. 115.   37. Ibid., p. 124.

think of him, since that is, in large part, how good he
is."38

As the language of the materials just quoted suggests,
Caplow and McGee's diagnosis of the academic marketplace in the late 1950s was cynical and denunciatory in
tone. The basis for this tone, moreover, lay in their conviction that the recruiting system minimized information
about candidates' real qualities, and ran on subjective
judgments about candidates that circulated selectively from
sponsors to hiring departments. That tone was further
sharpened by their conviction that subjective judgments by
prestigious sponsors bore little or unknown correspondence
to any valid assessment of the genuine excellence of the
candidate; after all, such judgments are *subjective* and not
objectively measurable. Holding such assumptions, they
had to conclude that such a market process was arbitrary
and unjust, because it deviated from the legitimate values
of universalistic assessment of excellence and promise in
research and teaching, and relied, moreover, on "mere"
prestige. Had they relaxed those informing assumptions,
their judgment might not have been so harsh. Had they
assumed that recommendations by sponsors were not an
exclusive alternative to judgments based on knowledge,
but rather a shorthand form of knowledge that is relied
upon when exact knowledge is impossible to attain, their
outrage might have diminished. Had they assumed further
that sponsors' recommendations on candidates were based
on years of experience in working with them as students or
colleagues, they might have regarded such recommendations as a more reliable and efficient means of gaining knowledge about the candidates than evaluating them
directly. And had they assumed that sponsors were motivated to provide frank and reliable recommendations to
safeguard their own reputations as professionals adhering to
high standards of excellence, they might have regarded the
network of personal influence as a reliable and efficient

38. Ibid., p. 128.

mechanism for allocating individuals with varying talents to and from institutions of varying quality.

We also note a related problem in Caplow and McGee's analysis: their tendency to take an "either-or" view of the relations between the criteria of personal contacts and influence networks. More realistically, these sets of criteria should be regarded as sometimes supplementary and capable of combination in various ways. The following possibilities come to mind:

1. Conducting a search that conforms to Caplow and McGee's "model hiring situation." This involves a completely public and exhaustive search for candidates, generating a pool containing *all* potentially qualified candidates, which would then be evaluated, case by case, in accord with universalistic criteria for achievement and promise of achievement.

2. Conducting a complete and exhaustive public search of the sort just mentioned, but *supplementing* it by contacting the various members of one or more professional networks (chairpersons of graduate training centers, professional colleagues). This involves an effort to expand the pool of candidates and to give salience to those that can be produced by known or trusted sources. This is not to say that the supplementary, informal search does not emphasize universalistic criteria—often it does—but it does move away from the picture of completeness, exhaustiveness, and fairness associated with the "model hiring situation."

3. Conducting a search without public advertisement, but making an effort to exhaust the relevant networks. This might take the form of writing all chairpersons of all graduate training programs in the country, and securing a list of candidates and their credentials. This would exclude those candidates that are not known in those networks.

4. Conducting a search by contacting only selective, "prestige" institutions that are reputed to produce the best qualified candidates.

5. Contacting only prestige institutions, *and* relying only on the recommendation of influential persons in those institutions.

6. Appointing a *given person* who has been mentioned by an influential figure as being "the best" or "the most promising" available. The empirical picture characterized by Caplow and McGee in the late 1950s stressed these last two variations.

The relations between "universalistic" and "personal" or "network" criteria, moreover, are variable, not fixed. Reliance on the recommendations of personal sponsors as a basis for recruitment opens the possibility that criteria which are alternative to, or opposed to, or contradictory with universalistic criteria of achievement and promise are being invoked in the recruitment process; it also opens up the possibility that better-qualified candidates are being excluded from consideration. We stress the term, "possibility," however, and emphasize that possibility does not imply necessity. It is also a possibility that a search relying mainly on recommendations of influential and outstanding colleagues would yield essentially the same—or even better—results as a public search, if universalistic criteria are consistently invoked in the process. Finally, we would argue that the two sets of criteria would vary from *individual search to individual search* in the degree to which they would supplement, oppose, or contradict one another as principles of recruitment.

Caplow and McGee concluded their study with a number of recommendations for change, among which were the following:

That procedures for locating candidates to fill vacancies be improved by increasing the amount of available information about those positions.

That regular, orderly procedures can be established for selecting new faculty members from a roster of candidates.

That a faculty vacancy be defined always on the basis of

demonstrated need for a particular position, "never on the basis of automatic succession."[39]

Certainly these recommendations are consistent with the diagnosis that Caplow and McGee ventured. Furthermore, they mark an effort to move away from what the authors regarded as the existing preferential system toward the "model hiring situation" in which information is maximized, universalistic standards of excellence are applied, and particularistic or personal influence is minimized. In many respects, Caplow and McGee were reaffirming traditional academic values of excellence; their complaint was that these values were being corrupted by relying on shortcuts and personal influence. Their recommendations foreshadowed a number of pressures to change the process of academic recruitment that actually developed in the late 1960s and the 1970s. Those recommendations proved to be directly relevant to the kinds of procedures that we attempted to build into our search at Berkeley in 1975–76.

Networks of personal influence will reappear in the story of our own search, and we will evaluate them generally at the conclusion of our report and analysis. At this point, we note only that they constitute a complicating factor in the academic market and represent an additional source of deviation from classical economic assumptions about market processes.

4. *Alternative Criteria for Recruitment: Discrimination and Affirmative Action*

For many decades advocates for various disadvantaged groups—mainly ethnic minorities and women, but other groups as well, such as aged, disabled, or handicapped persons—have protested against market discrimination, which both constitutes and reproduces their condition of

39. Ibid., p. 253.

disadvantage. Until recent decades, however, most of that protest focused on *direct* discrimination, that is, the deliberate exclusion of people from categories of employment on the basis of color, sex, age, or some other ascribed characteristic.

Concern with direct discrimination has continued to the present time, but in recent decades another type of concern has assumed greater salience: even under circumstances when deliberate, direct exclusion of disadvantaged persons from employment is not evident, discrimination continues to occur through the routine application of criteria that heretofore have been regarded as perfectly legitimate. To select perhaps the best-known example, evaluating individual children on the basis of objective "intelligence tests" that are constructed in such a way that minority or lower-class children will score lower on them because of their cultural experience may constitute, in effect, a way of discriminating against those children. The same kinds of complaints can be made with respect to admission for graduate academic study and recruitment. Reliance on traditional criteria of academic performance—such as scores on aptitude tests, grades in mathematics classes, and grades in college courses—for admission to graduate study in effect discriminates against those who, in the past, either have been discouraged from excelling academically or who have been directly discriminated against. Or again, hiring for academic positions by relying on the recommendations of influential colleagues may exclude from consideration talented but less visible disadvantaged candidates and thus constitute discrimination against them.

The guiding philosophy of much of "affirmative action" is rooted in the considerations just reviewed. That philosophy calls for an active assault on those practices and procedures which have heretofore operated to exclude disadvantaged groups, and thereby to increase the proportions of those groups in categories of employment in which they have been underrepresented. Affirmative action policies, moreover, introduce an alternative to relying on traditional universalistic criteria in recruiting. As in our consideration of personal networks, we should stress the word "alternative"; affirmative action may imply a number of different policies or strategies, not all of which compete with or are opposed to traditional universalistic criteria. To illustrate, consider the following procedures, all of which have been practiced in the name of affirmative action:

1. To conduct a public search and supplement it with special efforts to generate candidates from heretofore disadvantaged groups, while adhering to the application of universalistic achievement criteria in assessing all candidates. An example of this would be to request a list of all black sociologists from the membership roster of the American Sociological Association and to mail a copy of the announcement of an opening to each of them. This form of affirmative action does not necessarily assure the inclusion or appointment of previously disadvantaged groups, but only encourages their appearance in the pool of candidates. Moreover, it can be completely consistent with the evaluation of candidates in terms of universalistic criteria of academic achievement.

2. To select a candidate from a disadvantaged group when two or more candidates appear to be equally well qualified on universalistic criteria of achievement and promise. While often practiced, this procedure is difficult to apply unambiguously, because of the problem—not only in a field like sociology, but generally—of deciding that two or more candidates are equally qualified in some measurable way.

3. To select a candidate from a disadvantaged group when he or she appears to be *less* well qualified—by criteria of academic achievement and promise—than candidates from advantaged groups. Often this policy is legitimized by giving greater weight to some other criteria not traditionally observed—criteria such as "community experience," for example—and thereby defining the

selected candidate as equally or better qualified on grounds of those other criteria.

4. To restrict a recruitment search by *reserving* a position for a member of a disadvantaged category and actively excluding other candidates from consideration. This is the strongest form of affirmative action, and involves direct discrimination in favor of one group against another by invoking particularistic criteria. Universalistic criteria even may enter this most extreme case, however, if an effort is made to appoint the best qualified person in the disadvantaged category.

A MODEL FOR RECRUITMENT AS A
SUCCESSION OF EXCLUSIONS

To develop a model of the recruitment process, we begin by imagining a completely open, universalistic search. This calls for the systematic application of objective standards of evaluation and for an exhaustive and openly conducted search for talent. If such a search were to contain minimum restrictions on those who might apply, an advertisement for the relevant position would have to read something like, "Wanted: Sociologist," with an address for response that does not identify the recruiting institution. Such generality would be necessary if the maximum number of candidates were to be generated. In the actual selection process, all applicants would be treated as equals, and would be evaluated thoroughly and fairly. In its pure form, also, the evaluation would be blind, without reference to the candidate's name or other identifying characteristics that might bias the evaluation of his or her actual career and promise.

Such a search is obviously fictional, for a number of reasons. In a field like sociology, the objective application of universalistic criteria is clouded by three ambiguities. The first concerns *which* criteria are defined as relevant to universalistic evaluation: is it written work, evidence on teaching, evidence of special skills (such as language, quantitative methods), "experience" in interesting and important social situations, or something else? The second ambiguity concerns the level of agreement on the criteria for excellence. Can a given candidate be regarded as excellent with regard to, for example, published research, and can consensus be gained on the definition of excellence? Third, there is an ambiguity with respect to the judgment of promise, which always entails a bet on future performance. What are the bases for determining an individual's promise, and can consensus be reached on these?

Another reason why the completely open, universalistic model we have sketched is fictional is that, in the course of search and selection, certain categories of individuals are systematically excluded on the basis of a categorical judgment on the part of both recruiters and candidates. Not all of these judgments, moreover, are made on universalistic grounds. Indeed, the entire process may be regarded as the successive application of criteria for exclusion, so that in the last analysis only one candidate for the position remains. The character of the search, moreover, is revealed by *which* criteria are used for exclusion, what weight is given to each criterion, and what subset of candidates is excluded by the application of each.

These criteria of exclusion are:

1. The limitation of certain administrative and budgetary specifications laid down by the recruiting institution. Institutions often insist that candidates be holders of a Ph.D., which excludes people holding lower degrees in sociology, and also, for the most part, those holding degrees in academic fields other than sociology. Recruiting institutions also typically specify the rank at which the appointment is to be made. At the present time, for example, most recruitment is restricted to the junior, non-tenured levels. If such is the policy, a large number of potential candidates who are older and of higher rank are

excluded from consideration. Finally, recruiting institutions usually identify, in their search, one or more sub-
fields of sociology (family, stratification, theory) in which
the appointment will be made. Depending on how tightly
such subfields are defined, a greater or lesser number of
potential candidates are excluded because they do not fall
into appropriate subfields. By virtue of these various specifications, the vast majority of persons who could respond
to the general "want ad" for a sociologist are excluded
before the search actually begins.

2. The conditions and decisions emanating from potential candidates themselves. Some potential candidates may
not see a public advertisement, even though it is widely
disseminated. Among those candidates who actually know
of the available position, a large proportion "self-select"
themselves out of the running by not applying. They may
do this because they do not wish to move to the region
where the institution is located; because they have a negative image of the advertising institution; because their
interests and abilities do not match those specified in the
job description; because they believe that the competition
for the position will be too stiff and they have no reasonable chance for success; or for any other reason. It is always
difficult to measure the degree to which self-selection out
of a competition occurs, because such decisions are often
unconsciously arrived at and never systematically recorded.

3. The assessments of the candidates' qualifications
based on universalistic criteria.

4. The assessments of the candidates' qualifications by
known, trusted, or influential colleagues.

5. The consideration of candidates' racial, ethnic, sex-
ual, religious, or nationality characteristics.

We have now identified five bases for excluding candidates who are being considered for appointment. We believe that the first two are by far the most important. At
the present time, these five criteria differ according to the

degree to which they are held to be legitimate; moreover, different politically significant groups vary according to the degree to which they regard each as legitimate. It is generally believed to be legitimate for an institution to specify the number and rank of the positions it intends to fill, and to give some indication of the special fields of interest it intends to emphasize in screening candidates. Certainly, also, self-selection is widely regarded as a legitimate process. Whether or not a candidate decides to apply for a given position is considered to be his or her own business, and no one seriously argues that potential candidates be *required* to apply for a given position. The legitimacy of the remaining three sets of criteria, however, is at the present time subject to serious ideological conflict and debate.

Furthermore, the *basis* on which one set of criteria is held to be illegitimate in any degree is that it contravenes the application of another which is regarded to have greater legitimacy. To illustrate, if a department of sociology specifies that it wishes to fill several positions in demography, with emphasis on quantitative methods and mathematical models, this specification could be challenged on the grounds that it would systematically exclude minorities and women, who traditionally have not followed mathematically-oriented lines of specialization. It could be argued further that other kinds of subfields—such as sociology of sex roles or race relations—might skew the emphasis in the opposite direction. To illustrate again, the grounds on which the application of affirmative-action criteria are often attacked is that they undermine the application of universalistic criteria of achievement. Finally, reliance on personal influence is often regarded to be illegitimate, both because it likely excludes highly qualified candidates by restricting the search (thereby contravening the application of universalistic academic criteria), and because it likely excludes minority groups and women, who are not as visible to members of a collegial network. These illustrations show that the various criteria are always in potential conflict with one another. In fact, most of the contemporary debate over recruitment in the academic market involves conflicting assertions by different groups that different criteria be given higher or lower priority in the process of recruitment.

CHAPTER 2

Market Dynamics: Selected
Theoretical and Historical Themes

The market for academic research and graduate training as
a whole has meager powers of adapting to changing economic and social conditions. Some of the factors outlined
in the preceding chapter will be seen to have implications
for that lack of adaptability.

Primarily theoretical considerations will be discussed
first in this chapter, followed by an examination of the
changes during the past two decades in the academic
market in general and in the market for sociologists in
particular. We describe the relevant characteristics of the
environment as of the middle part of the 1970s, during
which our recruitment story unfolded. For this reason our
analysis will be selective, and we make no effort to produce
a general theoretical or historical analysis.

SOME DYNAMIC PRINCIPLES

In many respects the academic "industry" is a self-supplying one in the sense that most who found employment
in it do so in the same category of institution that "produced" them. This is true for the academy as a whole;
about 60 percent of the nation's Ph.D.'s end up in aca-

demic employment.[1] It is even more so for sociology as a discipline, in which approximately three-quarters of those receiving Ph.D.'s are employed in academic institutions.

In part as a result of this phenomenon of self-supply, the demand for academic services is similar to the demand for investment goods in the economy generally. Cartter describes that demand as follows:

[The demand for college teachers] is largely a "derived demand," depending on the rate of change in the total number of students attending college. Thus, if the ratio of students to faculty remains constant at, say, 15 to 1 and total enrollment moves from 5 million to 5,150,000 one can expect that about 10,000 new teachers will be required to handle the additional students. However, if instead of a 3 percent increase in enrollment there is a 6 percent increment, the total of new teachers required to handle new enrollments would rise by 100 percent. Therefore, like the case of investment goods, small changes in the demand for final products (the education of students) produces an exaggerated change in the demand for investment inputs (college teachers). Fairly significant swings in the demand for new academic personnel must be expected in the academic labor market.[2]

To round out that statement, we should add that with decreases in college enrollment the downward movement in demand for college teachers is equally precipitous, and that the "investment industry" (graduate training centers) may face problems of excess capacity.

The ability of the academy to respond to fluctuations of this sort is limited because of the long gestation period for producing a Ph.D. As we noted earlier, the process takes

1. Allan M. Cartter, "The Academic Labor Market," in Margaret S. Gordon (ed.), *Higher Education and the Labor Market* (New York: McGraw-Hill, 1974), p. 282. Of the remainder, more than two-thirds are dependent upon federal expenditures. Cartter added that both these sources are subject to considerable fluctuation.
2. Allen Cartter, *Ph.D.'s and the Academic Labor Market* (New York: McGraw-Hill, 1976), p. 2.

from three to ten years. Among academic disciplines, moreover, sociology is among the highest in terms of number of years lapsed between entry into graduate school and completion of degree.[3] Even if graduate-training centers are responsive to market conditions, a long period of time elapses between decisions on the part of university and departmental administrations to expand, on the one hand, and the appearance of the Ph.D. on the market on the other. By the latter time, moreover, the demand situation originally responded to may have changed again.

The responsiveness of supply is further complicated by the fact that suppliers (universities and graduate training centers) are attuned to conditions other than economic demand when they make their decisions to expand or contract the level of Ph.D. output. Earlier we argued that among the dominant forces in the "utility function" of colleges and universities is the motivation to enhance their general academic prestige. One of the principal ways to do this is to develop ambitious graduate training programs and research complexes. This strategy of expansion may coincide with demand needs when the market is in a state of expansion, but under stationary or declining demand for college teachers, expansion in the interests of improving institutional prestige may run counter to economic indications. This kind of situation is difficult to control, moreover, since there is no real national administrative manpower plan for academics, and decisions to expand or contract graduate training are localized in departments, university administrations, boards of trustees, and state governments.

The factors just mentioned make for serious rigidities in adjusting supply to demand conditions in the academic market. In addition, the academy possesses a number of structural characteristics that make it difficult to reduce

3. Neil J. Smelser and James A. Davis (eds.), *Sociology: Outlook and Needs* (Englewood Cliffs, N.J.: Prentice-Hall, 1968), Chapter 8.

the existing size of the educational establishment. The first has to do with its mode of financial support. Except for private institutions, most "firms" in the academy are not threatened with the prospect of "going out of business"— in the sense of going bankrupt—when demand for their services slacks off or declines. They are sustained by some sort of public purse—which, to be sure, may be adjusted downward in hard times—but it is difficult if not impossible politically to conceive of the possibility of closing down large numbers of public institutions. And although it is possible in principle to eliminate various sorts of advanced training programs under conditions of reduced demand, the persons in charge of such programs can throw enormous political obstacles in the way of this change.

Perhaps most important among the sources of inflexibility is the institution of tenure. As a large portion of the faculty of an institution becomes "tenured in," it becomes increasingly difficult to reduce its size in times of low demand for their services. Most institutions prefer to think in terms of modest measures such as freezes on new hirings, encouraging early retirements, increasing the academic workload, and the like—though these are of limited effectiveness in the short run.

These several factors underscore the paradoxical market situation of the academy. It is likely to be weakly responsive to changing manpower needs. In periods of rapid increases in demand it cannot respond quickly; and in periods of slackening demand it is difficult to reduce its level of output. The research-and-graduate-training component of higher education is likely to be forever behind in the race to catch up with the increased demand, and is likely to discover repeatedly that when it appears to have caught up, it has overshot the mark. It is a striking instance of the "cobweb effect," in which the investment industry is always out of equilibrium with the industry it supplies.

SOME HISTORICAL MARKET TRENDS

The general historical picture for higher education in the past three or four decades has been influenced most decisively by two sets of conditions: war and demographic phenomena. After World War II there was an enormous flood of veterans into the colleges and an exaggerated demand for teachers of all kinds. This wartime-generated demand more than compensated for what would have been much lower college enrollments traceable to the lower birthrates of the early 1930s. The demands for education by World War II veterans began to fall off dramatically in the early 1950s, however, and it was sustained only partially by the flow of Korean War veterans to the college campus; moreover, the effect of the lower birthrates in the depression years began to be felt. According to Cartter's assessment, the 1950s were uneasy years for higher education. The high birthrates of the decade encompassing World War II and the ensuing years promised great increases of enrollment in the very late 1950s and 1960s, but in the meantime enrollments were low, and some private institutions in financial trouble were seeking absorption into developing public systems. Between 1953 and 1963, there was an increase in the proportion of faculty members holding the doctorate in colleges and universities, suggesting that supply was slightly higher than demand in those years.[4]

The 1960s, as anticipated, brought great increases in enrollment, with an average increase of almost 8 percent between 1957 and 1967 (falling to a more modest 4 percent after 1967). During those years a serious shortage of college teachers developed, and, in response, graduate training centers began to expand their programs, faculties, and facilities to meet the crisis.[5] But, in characteristic

4. Cartter, *Ph.D.'s and the Academic Labor Market*, pp. 11–17.
5. Ibid., p. 1.

fashion, by the time that this growth in graduate training
had reached its full momentum, the rate of growth of
demand for its "products" had begun to slacken. Fields
such as physics and mathematics were experiencing some
difficulties in placing recent doctorates as early as 1967 and
1968, and others also did so, with varying intensity, in the
following two years. However, supply continued to zoom
upward. Between 1968 and 1974, "doctorates awarded
grew by 10,600 (46 percent) and first-year enrollments in
graduate programs expanded by 155,000 (34 percent); the
number of universities awarding the doctorate grew by
more than 40 between 1968 and 1974, and many additional doctoral programs were initiated that had not yet
awarded a degree by 1974."[6] By 1973 it was generally
evident that the imbalances between supply and demand
were extremely serious, and that, given long-term birth-
rate and other demographic trends, were likely to continue
so for several decades to come.

Among those demographic trends is one specific to the
academy itself. During the period of extremely rapid
growth in enrollments in the late 1950s and the 1960s,
most institutions responded by recruiting and promoting
to tenure larger numbers of faculty members. The net
effect of this was to generate an unusually large cohort of
young, tenured faculty members in those years. That
cohort, because it is tenured, has not diminished notably
in size as the rate of growth in enrollment has slowed and
the demand for college teachers has declined. Rather, it
has continued to move slowly through the academic life
cycle. Now in its late forties and fifties and in the high
salary ranges of the full professoriat, that cohort constitutes
a large fixed cost for colleges and universities and has
contributed in part to the rising costs of higher education.
Furthermore, the fact that so few in this cohort have
resigned, retired, or died contributes to the relatively low
replacement needs now being experienced by many institu-

6. Ibid., p. 21.

tions of higher education. The rigidities created by this cohort promise to ease in the 1980s and 1990s when large numbers will leave the academic system through retirement or death, thus increasing demand somewhat. But for the next decade or two, that cohort constitutes an aggravation to the oversupply situation occasioned more generally by the declining growth rates of enrollment and the increased supply of Ph.D.'s.

The historical swings in the academic market for sociologists have been similar. Writing in 1964, Ferriss drew the following picture:

During the 1930s the "problem" of sociological manpower, if any, was one of oversupply. During the war years those capable of special services in government, military, and public life, allocated themselves to productive positions, and there was little time for training sociologists. After World War II, commonplace shortages in all areas of life led to no great concern over sociological manpower; in any event, the onslaught of students entering graduate school brooked well for the future. Graduate enrollments and the number achieving the doctorate in sociology have since declined, but the demand for sociologists has expanded, giving rise to a problem in sociological manpower.[7]

The "problem" he was referring to was an anticipated shortage of doctorates in sociology for the next seven or eight years. He saw an increase in course offerings, in the number of departments of sociology, in the number of institutions of higher education, and in the number of students enrolled in colleges and universities—all pointing to a continuing increase in demand. He supplemented these estimates by pointing out that more "applied" sociologists would be demanded by professional schools and governmental agencies. Finally, he saw new technological changes providing more demand for sociologists, as well as foreign needs for demographers and other special-

7. Abbott L. Ferriss, "Sociological Manpower," *American Sociological Review*, Vol. 39 (1964), pp. 103–104.

ists.[8] Similar diagnoses and projections appeared throughout the 1960s.[9]

As in the remainder of the academy, sociology graduate training centers began, with a lag, to produce doctorates in greater numbers. In 1960–61, the nation's universities granted 184 Ph.D. degrees in sociology, and that figure grew consistently and steadily to a number of 534 one decade later;[10] a separate estimate for 1972 indicated that 555 new Ph.D.'s were seeking employment.[11] As far as demand was concerned, the year 1971–72 appeared to mark a somewhat dramatic turning point, with a slight increase in Ph.D.'s seeking employment in that year, but a marked decline of new positions from 1600 in 1971 to 883 in 1972. Projecting the trends, Finsterbusch estimated that the declining demand curve would cross the rising supply curve by 1973 or 1974.[12] Longer-term estimates led to predictions of "a steadily worsening manpower situation," and a forecast by Robert McGuiness based on survey data predicted an "underemployment" rate of 17 to 25 percent of all sociologists.[13]

In 1973 the Executive Office of the American Sociological Association conducted a survey of forty-one universities ranked in American Council on Education surveys, asking them to indicate the relative difficulty of "placing" graduate students as compared with one year earlier. Of the total, nineteen indicated it was more difficult, twenty

8. Ibid., p. 109.

9. See, for example, the projection for a "cumulative deficit" of sociologists, based partly on additional estimates by Ferriss and reported by the Behavioral and Social Sciences sociology panel. Smelser and Davis (eds.), *Sociology: Outlook and Needs,* Chapter 8.

10. "How Many are We?" *The American Sociologist,* Vol. 7, No. 8 (October 1972), p. 8.

11. Kurt Finsterbusch, "The Rise and Fall of the Academic Job Market for Sociologists," *The American Sociologist,* Vol. 7, No. 10 (December 1973), p. 3.

12. Ibid., p. 4.

13. Karen J. Winkler, "Few Openings: Sociologists Still in Demand, but Job Outlook is Clouded," *Footnotes,* Vol. 1, No. 8 (November 1973).

said it was the same, and two indicated that it was less difficult.[14] As a matter of personal recollection, we estimate that in placing graduate students from Berkeley to other institutions, the year 1972 or 1973 marked the time at which we began to grow apprehensive about students' chances, writing more letters of recommendation for them, and widening the range of institutions to which we advised them to apply. Thus, while it is very difficult on the basis of existing information to pinpoint the exact moment at which the conditions of oversupply began to surface, it is clear that those conditions were a definite social—and social-psychological—fact by 1975–76, the year when we initiated our search.

THE RISE OF AFFIRMATIVE ACTION

The 1960s were years of unprecedented political turmoil in American higher education. Much of the impetus for this turmoil was generated by students' demands for educational reform and greater student power, as well as the society-wide protest against American involvement in the Vietnam war which was spearheaded by the colleges and universities. In addition, particularly in the late 1960s and early 1970s, colleges and universities came under intense pressure to take direct action—mainly in the form of admissions and recruitment practices—that would work toward righting the discriminatory wrongs suffered by various minority groups and women over the past decades.

That pressure manifested itself in a variety of forms. As increasing numbers of minority groups were admitted into undergraduate and graduate schools, group after group formed caucuses that exercised pressure on academic departments and central administrations to sustain or increase that level of admissions, to recruit additional minority

14. Kurt Finsterbusch, "The 1973 Academic Job Market for Sociologists," *Footnotes*, Vol. I, No. 8 (November 1973).

faculty and staff members, and to establish academic programs with specific attention to minority studies.
Women's caucuses also formed and began to exert similar
demands on their own behalf. Political and economic pressures from the federal government complemented the efforts of those organized groups, In particular, the Department of Health, Education, and Welfare began insisting
on certain practices on the part of many universities—such
as preparing "targets" for increasing proportions of minority and women members of the faculty and staff, changing
recruitment procedures so as to identify larger numbers of
qualified minorities and women, and the like—on pain of
being denied substantial amounts of research funds from
that agency.

Professional associations also experienced the pressure for
affirmative action. Minorities and women in the American
Sociological Association, for example, formed vocal caucuses and began pressing demands for affirmative action on
to the agendas of the Council of that Association. Partly in
response to those demands, the Association took such steps
as permitting these groups a more significant place on the
programs of the annual meetings, appointing a staff
member in the Executive Office with specific responsibilities to deal with issues relating to minorities and
women, and establishing a program of fellowships for
minority graduate students. In addition, the pages of the
two "house-organ" publications of the Association—*The
American Sociologist* and *Footnotes*—began to show increasing study and debate on the fate of minorities and
women in the profession.[15] And though such pressure for

15. For a sample of research and debate on these topics, see Maurice
Jackson, "Minorities and Women in Sociology: Are Opportunities Changing?"
The American Sociologist, Vol. 7, No. 8 (1972), pp. 3–5; Jose Hernandez,
Jay Strauss, and Edwin Driver, "The Misplaced Emphasis on Opportunity for
Minorities and Women in Sociology," *The American Sociologist,* Vol. 8, No.
3 (1973), pp. 121–126; Barbara R. Lorch, "Reverse Discrimination in Hiring
in Sociology Departments: A Preliminary Report," *The American Sociologist,*
Vol. 8, No. 3 (1973), pp. 116–20; Bart Barnes, "Reverse Bias Alleged in
College Hiring," *Footnotes,* May 1973, p. 4; Daryl Chubin, "Sociological

affirmative action policies in the academy may have been abated somewhat by the mid-1970s, such pressure was still very much in evidence and had established itself as one of the competing criteria for recruitment.

We mentioned earlier a kind of paradox of the market for research and graduate-training services—a paradox constituted by the tendency for supply adjustments to lag behind changes in demand and to overshoot those changes. We might now also note a second paradox in the relations between the historical changes in the academic market and rise of affirmative action. It might be argued plausibly— though speculatively, since the appropriate historical evidence is not available—that *one* of the factors contributing to the political affirmative-action pressures on the colleges and universities in the 1960s lay in the general sense of opportunity engendered by the massive expansion of higher education during that decade. Whether or not this was the case, it is certainly clear that political consciousness among minorities and women surged in the late 1960s, and that this consciousness manifested itself in vigorous demands for greater representation in the faculties and staffs of colleges and universities. Yet it was at precisely the historical moment that these demands reached a point of political articulation that the opportunities to accommodate them—through increased hiring of minorities and women—began to dwindle. That dwindling, moreover, was the result of a general decline in demand for college and university personnel, with the consequence that it became difficult to expand the numbers of *any* category of faculty or staff—minority or majority, women or men. Pressing this reasoning further, we might suggest that the apparent reduction in affirmative-action pressure on the part of minorities and women in the mid-1970s was partially the result of the general *lack* of opportunity in the

Manpower and Womenpower: Sex Differences in Career Patterns of Two Cohorts of American Doctorate Sociologists," *The American Sociologist*, Vol. 9, No. 2 (May 1974), pp. 83–92.

academy, which itself was a product of extreme conditions of oversupply that developed in the early 1970s and promised to continue for decades. Finally, to carry this reasoning to its speculative extreme, we might posit a certain "cobweb effect" that obtained—political demands lagged behind economic opportunities, and the two tended to be continuously out of equilibrium.

CHAPTER 3

Organizational Responses
to the New Market Conditions

When the new market conditions outlined in the preceding chapter are translated into concrete exigencies for academic departments in universities, these exigencies assume the following three forms. First, from the standpoint of recruitment and placement, there is greater difficulty experienced by departments in securing "slots" for new appointments and in placing their own new Ph.D.'s in positions. Second, for those positions that do open, departments are faced with a much greater burden of work in filling them, mainly because of having to process the large numbers of applicants for each position. Third and finally, departments are under varying degrees of pressure from within and without to pursue the goals of affirmative action and increase the numbers of previously excluded minorities and women. How have departments responded to these pressures? Have there been any systematic responses on the part of the profession as a whole?

To throw light on these questions we included a number of interviewing visits in our research. In the spring of 1977, Content visited the sociology departments of the following institutions: the University of Chicago, Columbia University, Indiana University, the University of Michigan, and the University of North Carolina. In choosing these institutions, we wished to include those that are

CHART 1

Comparative Figures from ASA Guide, 1976

	Berkeley	Chicago	Columbia	Indiana	Michigan	UNC
Graduate Students Admitted						
1973–74	32	46	39	27	28	13
1974–75	28	43	31	25	15	16
1975–76	26	50	44	22	31	19
Graduate Student Enrollment (1975–76)						
Full time	112	125	170	89	134	65
Part time	2	0	13	2	0	—
Degrees Granted (1974–75)						
M.A.	17	19	29	7	30	9
Ph.D.	19	22	14	7	29	15
Faculty (1975–76)						
Full time	23	15	17	32	30	19
Part time and joint appt.	4	7	8	8	11	7
TOTAL	27	22	15	40	41	26

comparable to Berkeley in size, academic standing, production of graduate students, and position in the market. Chart 1 provides some comparative data with respect to graduate admissions and enrollments, degrees granted, and size of faculty. While there is considerable variation among the six, all of them can be considered relatively large enterprises' according to these various measures; furthermore, all rank in the "top twenty" of the American Council on Education surveys. In her visits, Content interviewed chairpersons, members of personnel committees, placement officers, and non-faculty administrative assistants and clerical personnel. Her inquiries focused primarily on recruitment and placement procedures, with special reference to recent changes in these areas. These several institutions can scarcely be regarded as representing the entire academic scene. However, their experiences do provide us with some idea of the range of responses—at least of leading institutions—to the dramatically new market situation in which they have found themselves. To supplement these interviews, Smelser visited the executive offices of the American Sociological Association in Washington, D.C., in the fall of 1976, and interviewed several of its staff members with respect to any changes that the ASA had initiated in response to the changing academic market.

The discussion in this chapter is organized around the three sets of exigencies mentioned at the beginning, considering first the representative set of sociology departments we visited—including Berkeley for some of the comparisons—and next the ASA.

DIMINISHING RECRUITMENT AND INCREASING DIFFICULTY OF PLACEMENT

None of the departments we visited anticipated any significant growth of faculty in the forseeable future, though none foresaw a reduction either. The most common description of departmental circumstances was "steady state."

Most if not all faculty vacancies resulted from retirements (which are few in number, given the age structure of most faculties), from resignations (also few), and from denials of tenure. We gained the impression that tenure denials were the most frequent source of vacancies and, indeed, that promotion to tenure was becoming more difficult; at least, most of those we interviewed *believed* that to be the case. This certainly would be a plausible development, since in a buyer's market the buyer has the opportunity of being "choosier" and is likely to feel that one can afford fewer mistakes in appointment and promotion.

Under conditions of diminishing demand, economic logic would appear to dictate that steps be taken to reduce supply in some way. Yet we found little evidence that numbers in graduate programs have been curtailed by the sample of institutions we visited. While Chart 1 (p. 44) reveals some fluctuations in new admissions for each institution between 1973 and 1976, there is no downward trend. Our informants stressed the need for keeping enrollments high because of the need for research assistance from graduate students, and pointed out that while placing their students was becoming more difficult, very few of them actually went unplaced. One informant argued that the elite institutions definitely should *not* reduce their numbers of graduate students and Ph.D.'s granted, since that diminution would merely give lower quality institutions an opportunity to produce more Ph.D.'s. Our general impression from the interviews is that the size of graduate-department programs is dictated by conditions other than economic concerns. This squares with our earlier analysis of the general character of the academic market (in Chapter One).

An alternative to diminishing the supply of new Ph.D.'s is to become more systematic and aggressive in placing them. Every department officer who was interviewed expressed concern over placement of students, and most departments had instituted some machinery designed to make placement more effective, though in no case were innovations very dramatic. Columbia's and Berkeley's departments appeared to have changed least, maintaining a placement system that was both loose and decentralized. The placement officer served mainly as an information center (gathering lists of openings in other institutions and offering minimal advice and counseling to students). In both institutions students relied on those faculty members with whom they had worked closely to "sponsor" them on an individual basis. Occasionally the placement officer served as a kind of resort for those students who lacked influential faculty sponsors for one reason or another. In any event, little was done by the two departments as a whole to assist or encourage students.

The sociology departments at the University of North Carolina and the University of Michigan had adopted a system in the past several years which can be described as centralized but "open." The placement office served as a center of information, and provided helpful documents on "how to get a job" and other relevant advice. The students were expected to take the initiative in deciding where they wanted to apply and in informing the placement officer. Subsequently the latter sent out the curriculum vitae of the students along with a covering letter. Since, however, the placement officer did little by way of ranking or evaluating the student, the mechanism may have lost some effectiveness; such evaluative information is very important in the minds of recruiting institutions. At both Michigan and North Carolina the centralized system was introduced in response to student criticism that the individualized system of nomination by sponsors was inequitable. We also found some evidence of student dissatisfaction with the new system on grounds that it was not sufficiently "personalized" and that to include a student's curriculum vitae along with a number of others may not be the most forceful recommendation for a new Ph.D. seeking a place.

A third variant—centralized placement and nomination by the department as a whole—had been adopted by the sociology departments at the University of Chicago and

Indiana University. In these cases the placement officer played a key and powerful role. On the basis of a faculty poll, he or she determined who were the strongest applicants and which were to be nominated for the various openings in other universities. Those interviewed at Chicago and Indiana felt that the centralized nomination system provided more "clout" for the students, since they were nominated by the entire department, as it were. At the same time, they acknowledged that it was likely to generate dissatisfaction among those students who were not nominated for institutions to which they might want to apply. (It is true that they could apply on their own to any place, particularly if a "sponsor" would support them; but, still, some students may have experienced some kind of stigma at not being given top priority for nomination by the department as a whole.) It is also our impression that the centralized placement system would not be workable in departments with deep political and factional divisions, since consensus on "the best" students might be difficult to obtain.

Additional assistance to students seeking employment is spotty and informal. All the departments visited offered minimal services to former students by providing them with the listings of openings upon request. The University of North Carolina had adopted a conscious practice of having students give a preliminary presentation to a local audience before going out to an interview. A certain amount of this was done more informally at Chicago and Michigan, but not specifically as preparation for placement. Given the importance of the interview in determining the fate of applicants, this practice perhaps deserves emulation (see Chapter Six). However, we received little impression that other departments "coached" their candidates to any significant degree.

While a number of our informants expressed the belief that a greater proportion of Ph.D.'s will have to find non-academic positions in the future, very little effort was made in any of our sample institutions to explore those opportunities or press their students toward them. The dominant "culture" of the departments we visited was one in which the primary mission of a "quality" academic department should be to reproduce in graduate students the kinds of commitments and skills that the faculty themselves have, and hopefully to place those students in positions like those the faculty themselves hold. In the context of this culture both faculty and graduate students (if the latter are properly "socialized" by the faculty) considered jobs in the non-academic sector as a kind of last-resort alternative to attractive academic positions. This attitude, while probably becoming progressively more archaic in the changing academic market, nonetheless contributes to the unresponsiveness of academic units to the apparent need to place students outside the academy.

The final response to the situation of the diminishing recruitment opportunities and the increasing difficulty of placement was to "overload" the network. Concerned about their precarious career chances, students applied to more institutions and to a wider range of institutions in order to "cover their bases" in the uncertain market. This meant calling on faculty sponsors for more phone calls and letters of support. In conducting our own search, we uncovered much direct evidence of the burden placed on faculty members who, beleagured by students' requests, were attempting in various ways to systematize their sponsorship of graduate students.

Our general conclusion with respect to recruitment and placement, then, is that little was being done to alter the level of supply by individual graduate-training centers, and that equally little was being done to generate alternative sources of demand outside the academy. Formal and informal departmental responses with respect to placement were minor and incremental, and were designed mainly to improve the competitive situation of "one's own" within the confines of a traditionally defined market for academics.

COPING WITH THE WORK BURDEN
OF RECRUITMENT

As noted, one of the inevitable consequences of a tight and uncertain market is that more candidates will apply to more places, thus increasing the burden on the reviewers and recruiters in the hiring institution. Among the several adaptations that may be used to cope with this increased workload, the following come to mind: involving more faculty members in the personnel review process, to spread the work; involving graduate students in the review process, to achieve the same; drawing on the services of the non-academic staff; improving the "technology" of review and recruitment by installing superior reproducing equipment, automatic typewriters and so on; and hastening the review process by making it more cursory. To which of these adaptations had our selected institutions turned?

In all the institutions we visited, at least three faculty members were involved in the major review of candidates during a search, but in none did this constitute an *increase* in faculty involvement from times past. In most places at least two faculty members reviewed a candidate's curriculum vitae before he or she was eliminated from consideration. The one exception is the department at the University of North Carolina, where the chairperson of the personnel committee eliminated about half the candidates on his own, though he consulted with other faculty sometimes before doing so, and made all files available to any concerned faculty. At Chicago and Michigan the initial screening was done by a committee, but this committee simply served to weed out the weak cases and pass the remainder on to a stronger personnel committee or an executive committee. Chicago, a smaller department, had the greatest faculty involvement, since no candidate was asked to come for an interview until the full faculty agreed. At Indiana University and the University of Michigan, the actual hiring decision was not made by the full faculty but by an executive committee.

In all cases at least two graduate students were included in the search process, and in all but two cases (Chicago and Berkeley) graduate students were allowed on the committee to review letters of recommendation. In addition, graduate students attended in varying numbers the presentations made by visiting candidates, and usually had an opportunity to express their opinion to the faculty before a hiring decision was actually made. The main problem with graduate student participation did not appear to stem from any perceived threat to faculty power—as many faculty members have defined the issue in the past—but rather in student reluctance to undertake the work involved in reviewing the large number of candidates' files, a reluctance arising perhaps from their own sense of only peripheral involvement. In some cases a number of graduate students divided the work, and in one year the graduate students at the University of North Carolina did not even appoint a student member to the search committee.

With one exception, we could find no evidence of any attempt to increase the involvement of non-academic staff as a way of easing the burden of reviewing files. That exception was at Indiana University, where the chairperson's administrative assistant worked very closely with him, and was free of any supervisory or other responsibilities. She met regularly with the personnel committee to record its actions and prepared summary reports for the department chairperson. At other places the lack of secretarial assistance and increased paperwork were subjects of complaint, but little appeared to be done to alleviate the problems. In most cases departmental secretaries were assigned to a specific set of faculty members, and if one or more of them drew recruitment duty then the secretary was drafted, too. Normally, then, there was no continuity of involvement of a specific staff member with specific responsibility for matters of recruitment.

Similarly, we found virtually no evidence of the acquisition of supportive technology to facilitate the recruitment process. Indiana's department was again a partial exception, having been promised the use of an automatic typewriter on a sharing basis with all other departments in its building, and hoping to acquire the use of a computer. One institution made use of a word-processing center outside the department to duplicate letters of recommendation, and another duplicated letters of reference and typed in appropriate addresses. We found one department that was only in 1977 acquiring a photocopying machine!

This lack of response with respect to use of nonacademic staff and technological support may be attributed to lack of financial resources, since most of the departments we visited were required to finance their recruitment activities internally, except for funds to finance interviewing visits, which were normally provided by the university's central administration on a request basis. The low use of faculty and graduate students could be attributed to faculty and graduate students' reluctance to do the additional work and to faculty suspicion that graduate students are too heavily involved in departmental affairs. If, for whatever reasons, it is true that the departments we visited had made little use of these possible adaptations, in any of these areas, how had they responded to the increased demands on their time?

For the most part, the departments have simply streamlined the process of reviewing by adopting mechanisms to eliminate the large number of weak cases early and to concentrate on the careful evaluation and interview visits of the relatively few. One department deliberately adopted the policy of describing a vacancy in a quite specific and delineated way, in order to narrow the numbers of candidates who may have thought they belonged in the category as described. All had instituted some relatively superficial initial review, such as having one person screen for weak cases, having an initial "sorting" committee weed out weak candidates, or subdividing the labor of a personnel committee so that all members of the committee would not have to read every file. These decisions, moreover, were typically made on the basis of whatever the candidate submitted—usually a curriculum vitae alone. One department actually discouraged submission of anything more than a curriculum vitae at the early stages of a search. The only case in which an individual was requested to submit more than that was at the University of Chicago, at which letters of reference were sought for candidates who had been nominated by chairpersons at other institutions. When other materials accompanied the curriculum vitae, they were taken into account in the initial review.

The critical decisions for every hiring department were the selection of interviewees from the totality of candidates and the selection of appointees from the interviewees. The personnel committees at the University of North Carolina and Indiana University selected the individuals to be interviewed. The hiring decision was made by the full faculty at the University of North Carolina, Chicago, Columbia, and Berkeley; at Indiana and Michigan, the departments with the largest faculties, the decision on hiring was made by an executive committee elected by the faculty. Whatever the mechanism, however, faculty involvement in the process intensified during the visiting stage (which faculty members convened in varying numbers to hear formal presentations and to interview the candidate) and at the appointment stage. Furthermore, any lack of faculty involvement at these stages appeared not to stem from any direct and deliberate exclusion of faculty but rather to the burden of work required. It was difficult to expect that entire faculties would read candidates' materials in advance and attend formal presentations, particularly if a number of interviews were scheduled.

We have noted how very important the visit and interview of candidates is in the review process. We believe that this importance can be accounted for mainly by the strain on faculty time and the reluctance of departmental administrators to demand more of the faculty in the review process. Few faculty can or want to expend the time involved in a thorough review of all files or even the materials of the candidates being interviewed. They will be inclined, however, to take the hour or two to see candidates in person and base their preferences in large part on this kind of encounter. The importance of the interview, in short, is a reflection of the high level of faculty *non*-involvement in the earlier review of applications. Thus one of the unanticipated consequences of the increasing workload involved in recruitment may be a growing reliance on oral presentations rather than written work.

This account reveals that, at least for that small sample of institutions we visited, the departments had their backs to the wall in an era of limited departmental resources and experienced a great increase of work activity associated with the increasing numbers of applicants for any given opening. For the most part, these departments responded defensively, by speeding up the initial review to identify the strong candidates early and reduce the numbers quickly. While more ideal responses could be imagined, the departments' responses are understandable, given the circumstances of the market and the constraints on their own resources.

RESPONDING TO AFFIRMATIVE ACTION

In discussing affirmative action, it is essential to distinguish at once between the *results* of affirmative action—which are measured best by a department's actual performance in increasing the numbers of qualified minorities and women in its ranks—and the *procedures* by which these results are presumably attained. With respect to the former, the departments we visited (and our own as well) had succeeded in adding such persons to their ranks over the past several years. It is our impression, moreover, that sociology, by virtue of the disciplinary and ideological commitments of its practitioners, may be more self-consciously oriented to implementing the goals of affirmative action than many other academic disciplines.

With respect to affirmative-action procedures, however, our impression was a different and less sanguine one. These procedures mainly called for advertising a position widely and submitting a report to an agency of the university administration—perhaps an affirmative action office—which in its turn was prepared to pass it along to any external agencies who had an interest in the university's affirmative action policies and record. How did the institutions in our sample employ these procedures?

Most of the institutions we contacted advertised in the employment bulletin of the American Sociological Association. They acknowledged that this had been done only for the past three or four years, and that the practice was initiated to observe affirmative-action procedures. None, however, appeared to have made use of the placement service at the annual meetings of the American Sociological Association. All the institutions also wrote letters to departmental chairpersons and colleagues around the country, and included either affirmative-action language or non-discrimination language in the letter. The intent of the publicity was, of course, to make knowledge of the opening public, with the expectation that casting the net this widely would generate a larger pool of minority and women candidates.

All the departments we visited were also required to file some sort of report on their search activities. Generally these were narrative in character and did not require extensive supporting data. The main exception was a public institution, Indiana University, which exhibited the greatest amount of central administrative involvement in the search procedure. The department there was required to send a questionnaire to all candidates, calling for ethnic identity, but the questionnaire was to be returned to the campus affirmative-action office rather than the department, which never received the data. In addition, before a candidate could be brought for an interview at Indiana, the department had to obtain permission from the affirmative-action office. At the time that permission to interview was requested, that office reviewed the sex and ethnicity data they had collected. They could have used this data as a basis not to approve the interview. This considerable power to deny, however, had never been exercised with respect to a request from the sociology department for interviewing a candidate. At all the other institutions we visited, the affirmative-action office played a more passive role.

We believe that these procedures, which are insisted upon by affirmative-action offices, were almost totally ineffective in guaranteeing or even encouraging affirmative-action results (see Chapter Seven). They increased the necessary paperwork in two ways: first, by drawing in large numbers of applications in response to public advertisements, thus contributing to the heavy recruitment workload we have discussed; and, second, by calling for submission of additional paper to prove that the search was public and that all candidates were considered. Such advertising and reporting may be helpful in preventing grossly scandalous searches, but they do little to assure that special efforts to generate qualified minority and women candidates will be made by a department. Those special efforts would seem to arise more appropriately as a matter of commitment within a department and as a matter of financial support for augmented searches on the part of administrations. We shall return to this difficult issue when we undertake a general assessment and recommendations in the final chapter.

RESPONSES BY THE AMERICAN SOCIOLOGICAL ASSOCIATION

Earlier we noted that the American Sociological Association's official publications began to register alarm at the evidence of an apparently tightening market for academic sociologists in the early 1970s, and began considering possible solutions, such as expanding the opportunities for sociologists outside the academy, especially in government agencies, independent research agencies, and business. Recently the Association has undertaken certain measures to modify its own structure and procedures in order to devote more energy and perhaps more resources to the problems of job opportunities and placement for sociologists.

For some years the Association had a Committee on Employment of Sociologists, but on the whole it remained inactive. In 1976, partly out of concern for market conditions and partly in response to pressure from sociologists not employed in the academy, the Council of the Association changed the name of the committee to Committee on Expanding Employment Opportunities for Sociologists. Its chairperson and most of its members are non-academic sociologists. As of early 1977 the Committee had held several meetings but had not yet undertaken any major projects. In any event, that Committee will probably play a limited role, largely because of its limited funding by the Association.

In a related action, the Association upgraded the position of its Executive Specialist for Minorities and Women (a position created a number of years ago out of interest in affirmative action) to a higher-level position, entitled Executive Associate for Careers, Minorities, and Women. The change was motivated by the argument that progress with respect to the employment of minorities and women could not be expected without considering the broader issues of career opportunities in general. The incumbent is charged with spending the majority of time and energy in attempting to locate employment opportunities for sociologists. This involves securing and disseminating information, making informal contacts with employers— principally non-academic employers, we presume—and attempting to "educate" those employers as to what sociologists might have to offer to their particular kinds of organizations. The new position also serves as a staff liaison for the Committee on Expanding Opportunities for Employment of Sociologists.

The third instance of change, also relatively minor, had to do with streamlining the advertising procedures for openings that various employers want to list. Up to late 1976, employers used the ASA's *Footnotes,* published six times a year, as the medium for advertising positions. About that time, however, the decision was made to remove the advertisements from *Footnotes* and publish them separately in an Employment Bulletin, published monthly and sent by first-class mail. The motivation for publishing the information in a separate bulletin was to speed the turn-around time between submission of advertisements and their publication. It was anticipated that the new delay-time would be approximately one month, half of the previous delay-time. To cover costs, however, the Association required that those who received the employment bulletin must do so on a paid subscription basis. This operated to limit the publicity of positions only to those who actually subscribe, whereas *Footnotes* was mailed to every member as part of membership privileges.

Such are some of the efforts that the American Sociological Association initiated in response to changing market conditions for sociologists. It should be noted more generally, however, that the ASA is not likely to play a major role in facilitating the placement of sociologists in the various job markets, aside from providing a central information clearinghouse. That prediction is hazarded on the basis of the following considerations. As we have discovered and shall discover again (Chapters One and Seven) the existence of a collegial network, continuously sustained and renewed, is an extremely important facilitating resource in the placement of qualified academic personnel. In the academy that network is sustained partly through contacts with the activities of the professional associations, but the *operative* network processes in recruitment involve ties between colleagues in different academic institutions, since these institutions are the units that both produce and hire professional academics. The professional association is not, strictly speaking, part of that network, though it may contribute to its vitality.

With respect to the non-academic market for academics, the problem seems to be a more general one: the absence of any really effective network, at least for sociology. Traditionally, only one-quarter of sociologists have taken on non-academic positions subsequent to their training, and so on grounds of volume of recruitment alone, there is less interchange. More importantly, however, the relations between academic and non-academic sectors (government, business, law) are not sustained by a common range of activities that involve them in interaction with one another—activities such as attending conferences, reading one another's research, and indeed, placing one another's students. Up to the time of our interviews, there had been a certain amount of activity undertaken by the Executive Associate for Minorities and Women to make contacts with government agencies and business organizations, to acquaint them better with what sociologists can offer, and to encourage them to advertise in places that would be noticed by sociologists. Helpful in some degree, this activity tended, however, to be an isolated effort, lacking the built-in capacity for renewal that a collegial network has. It may be that with time and with an increase in the number of sociologists entering non-academic work some critical mass will be accumulated and some sort of network will begin to develop. But at the present time the absence of such a network greatly inhibits the effectiveness of the professional association.

As for placement itself, the American Sociological Association is also in a somewhat awkward position when it comes to doing more than providing information about candidates and openings. Many individuals send in a cur-

riculum vitae to the Executive Office in hopes of finding
academic placement, but the Executive Office staff does
not feel qualified or inclined to push these candidates
beyond making their availability known to those who
inquire. And since academic institutions do not normally
inquire from the ASA about available candidates, there is
very little interaction via the Executive Office between
employers and candidates. As for placement in non-
academic positions, the Executive Office periodically re-
ceives notification from a government agency or a business
firm that a position is available, but more often than not it
must be filled within a short period of time. Given the
academic contract, which is normally an annual one, most
qualified persons cannot be pried from their present positions within a short period of time. And since the ASA
Executive Office does not maintain rosters of available
"experts" for various kinds of positions, any kind of placement that results from these inquiries usually is based on
some knowledge that a staff member of the Executive
Office "accidentally" has at his or her fingertips at the time
the inquiry is made.

A CONCLUDING REMARK

Reviewing the presentation made in this chapter, it is not
difficult to conclude that the response among academic
sociologists to a really grave change in their market situation has been minimal. Little has been done to alter the
supply situation beyond increasing the competitiveness of
placement; little has been done by way of increasing the
energy and resources of recruitment efforts; and little has
been done to make the procedures of affirmative action
more relevant to the stated goals of affirmative action. It
would be easy, perhaps, to take a simply normative view of
this state of affairs and chastise sociologists—or academics
in general—for their apparent conservatism and reluctance

to respond. To stop at that, however, would be to misread the situation. The great demands for change being put on academic departments (and to a lesser extent, the professional association) call above all for an increase in the expenditure of resources. Yet these demands are being made in the context of a situation in which the administrative and political impulse is to restrict if not reduce the resources available to those very agents—academic departments—who are being called upon to expend more effort. The resulting situation is, in a word, impossible, and the only realistic response to be expected is that those agents will "make do" as best they can within the imposed limitations and constraints.

CHAPTER 4

Some Relevant Departmental History

In the eyes of most of those in the higher education establishment who make such judgments, the Department of Sociology at the University of California stands as one of the half-dozen leading centers of research and graduate training in the United States. It is commonly grouped— with some variation in actual institutions included—with Harvard, Columbia, and the Universities of Chicago, Michigan, and Wisconsin. Yet the historical route by which Berkeley's Department entered that group is unique. Almost all of the other currently leading centers were important sources of innovation in academic sociology during its formative years in the late nineteenth and early twentieth centuries, and each supplied at least one of the major founders or innovators in early academic sociology—Columbia's Franklin Giddings, Chicago's Albion Small, Michigan's Robert Cooley, and Wisconsin's Edward Allsworth Ross. (Harvard is an exception; sociology did not enter the scene there until the inter-war period.) By contrast, Berkeley did not even establish a department carrying the name of Sociology until 1946, almost a half-century after the great pioneering work had established centers of scholarship and teaching in sociology. Rather than building on established traditions, Berkeley's growth occurred afresh, as it were, after the discipline as a whole had won a measure of acceptance and legitimacy in the higher education establishment. To provide a selective background to our story of recruitment, we shall, in this chapter, select a few themes from its brief history.

On the Berkeley scene, too, sociology was a late arrival by comparison with the other social sciences. Anthropology was established as a department in 1901, economics in 1902, political science in 1903, and psychology in 1922. The academic unit that could be described as most nearly resembling sociology was established in 1919 as the Department of Social Institutions. This department endured until the 1940s, when the metamorphosis that ultimately resulted in a Department of Sociology began. The Department of Social Institutions was in many respects both the creation and the empire of Frederick Teggart, a renowned scholar who contributed substantively to the study of evolution and historical change during his years of active scholarship. Teggart was able, through recruitment and intellectual influence, to staff that small department with faculty members whose work reflected in varying degrees his own intellectual preoccupations. He and others on the campus were also successfully able to resist the introduction of a Department of Sociology as such—that is to say, a department which carried that name and which would be staffed by faculty members pursuing and teaching academic sociology as it was in other large university settings.[1]

After Teggart's retirement in 1941, various persons on the faculty and in the administration began contemplating the replacement, transformation, or expansion of the Department of Social Institutions. Resistance to sociology

1. For a series of reminiscences on Teggart's intellectual and personal qualities, see Robert Nisbet, "An Eruption of Genius: F. J. Teggart at Berkeley," *California Monthly* (April 1976).

continued in some quarters, however, and in the end a compromise was struck in 1946. That compromise was a department with the title of Sociology and Social Institutions—a title that reflected both the pressures for change and the pressures to resist change—with a professor of philosophy, Edward H. Strong, serving as a kind of caretaker chairman between 1946 and 1952.[2] During those years only a modest number of new appointments were made, and those were in areas that could be designated roughly as historical sociology. The decisive turn came in 1952, when Herbert Blumer, an established sociologist then at the University of Chicago, was recruited as new chairman of the small department with a mandate to expand.

1952–1964: THE ERA OF GROWTH

The dozen years following 1952 can be regarded as a kind of golden age of the growth of sociology at Berkeley. During that period the campus as a whole experienced perhaps the most dramatic period of growth and affluence in its entire history. The total enrollment of the campus almost doubled—from 15,630 in 1952 to 27,319 in 1964. The rate of growth of graduate students was even more dramatic, expanding from 3,972 in 1952 to 9,562 in 1964. Graduate students constituted 26 percent of the total student body in 1952; by 1964 it was 35 percent.[3] Furthermore, only at the end of that period did state officials begin to question the assumption that the state of California could sustain that kind of growth without seriously taxing its financial resources.[4] In the context of this general campus situation, the opportunities for a fledgling department were truly extraordinary.

2. The phrase "and Social Institutions" was dropped in 1961 after a unanimous departmental vote.

3. Neil J. Smelser, "Growth, Structural Change, and Conflict in California Public Higher Education, 1950–1970," in Smelser and Gabriel Almond (eds.), *Public Higher Education in California* (Berkeley: University of California Press, 1974), p. 81.

4. Ibid., pp. 21–22.

The growth of sociology in the dozen years after 1952 was also exceptional. In 1951, the year preceding Blumer's arrival, the Department of Sociology and Social Institutions had a cadre of only seven "ladder" faculty members—one full professor (the philosopher, Strong), three associate professors, and three assistant professors—along with an instructor and a lecturer. As a result of vigorous recruiting activities during the next twelve years, the total membership of the Department in 1964 came to 26 regular faculty members—fifteen full professors, four associate professors, and seven assistant professors—along with ten temporary appointees. Furthermore, the pattern of recruitment varied by rank and age. Of the nineteen ladder faculty members added between 1952 and 1964, eight were brought in at tenure rank by "raiding" senior scholars from other institutions. Of the remaining, eight were appointed as assistant professor (or on temporary appointment) and subsequently promoted to tenure. (Of the other assistant professors appointed between 1952 and 1964, two were not promoted to tenure, two resigned before a tenure decision was scheduled to be made, and the status of seven was not finally determined as of 1964.) Faculty members now remember the atmosphere of those years as one of expansiveness, optimism, and high morale. Perhaps such memories should be discounted for a nostalgia effect, but it should be pointed out that only one tenured faculty member was "stolen" from the Berkeley faculty, despite many efforts on the part of other institutions, and despite the general fact that those dozen years were the golden years of raiding as well.

Throughout the period the departmental emphasis was on improving the "quality" of the faculty—defined mainly in terms of excellence of published scholarly research. Indeed, it was Blumer's personal philosophy, stated explicitly on repeated occasions, to stress both quality and catholicity in building the faculty. That is to say, his emphasis was on securing "the very best" sociologists in the nation, attempting to build a department with a diversity of sociological styles and interests—as contrasted, for example, with a single dominant style such as quantitative-empirical sociology. This approach to recruitment gave much latitude to individual faculty members in the Department to press for the appointment of both young and senior scholars they believed to be promising or distinguished. In retrospect, we might speculate that this stress on catholicity and diversity constituted one of the bases for the number and depth of subsequent Departmental cleavages, to be described in the following chapter. Be that as it may, the Department was able to build itself in stature and reputation in those years of growth. In 1959, when the Keniston report on the prestige of graduate departments was published, Berkeley's department was accorded a rank of eighth in the nation.[5] Seven years later, when the Cartter report of the American Council on Education was published, Berkeley's department ranked first, both with respect to quality of graduate faculty and quality of graduate training.[6] In 1970, when the ACE published the results of a nearly identical poll, Berkeley retained its ranking as first in the nation, though in a virtual tie with Harvard's sociology department.[7]

1964–1974: CONFLICT,
RETRENCHMENT, AND AFFIRMATIVE ACTION

The year 1964 can be regarded as a terminal point for the golden era of growth in more than one sense. Beginning with the Free Speech Movement in the fall of 1964, the Berkeley campus as a whole was plunged into six or seven years of political turmoil that shook it profoundly. The

5. Hayward Keniston, *Graduate Education and Research in the Arts and Sciences at the University of Pennsylvania* (Philadelphia: University of Pennsylvania Press, 1959).

6. A. M. Cartter, *An Assessment of Quality in Graduate Education* (Washington: American Council on Education, 1966).

7. K. D. Rose and C. J. Andersen, *A Rating of Graduate Programs* (Washington: American Council on Education, 1970).

Sociology Department was among those departments most caught up in the turmoil, and on numerous occasions it polarized into a number of committed camps, each with a different posture toward student protest in general and toward the specific political issues associated with that protest. Many of the current political divisions in the Department still mirror stances taken during those years. In those same years, moreover, six tenured faculty members resigned from the Department and took positions in other institutions or in other departments on the Berkeley campus. Though the reasons for these departures were many and complex for each faculty member, a number of them specifically cited the politicized atmosphere of the Department as among the factors taken into account in their decisions. The Department recouped these losses in part by recruiting three senior scholars from other institutions, and in part by the appointment of additional assistant professors.

Simultaneously with this increased rate of turnover, the general rate of growth of departmental faculty began to slacken noticeably, and ultimately ceased altogether. As indicated, the Department had 26 regular faculty members in 1964. That number reached 28 in 1968, its largest number ever. The subsequent curtailment of growth was associated directly with the era of financial hardship initially imposed on the campus by the gubernatorial administration of Ronald Reagan in 1966, and continuing to the present time. In response to these financial stringencies, the administration adopted a number of new personnel policies. First, though no ladder faculty members were actually discharged, the vacancies occasioned by resignation, retirement, and non-promotion began to be recalled to the central administration and reallocated, not necessarily to the same department experiencing the vacancy. By this mechanism a department could actually be reduced in size over a period of years, though at a limited rate. Second, the campus administration, following something of a national trend, discouraged almost to a point of outright prohibition the appointment of faculty members at the tenured ranks. This policy was adopted as a way of economizing by making appointments at the lower salary ranges, and as a way of ensuring a flow of younger talent into a faculty that had, in the years of extremely rapid growth, become "top heavy" with tenured faculty as a result of promotions and senior appointments. As a result of these policies, the Department of Sociology's faculty personnel picture changed radically. Because the number of vacancies actually outnumbered the number of new appointments, the Department's total membership actually declined from its high of 28 in 1968–69 to 24 in the years 1970–73, then rose back to 26 in 1974–75. The last new appointment at the tenure level was in 1972.[8] By the early 1970s, moreover, the new economic realities had firmly established the expectation that, for the indefinite future, the best the Department could expect would be a kind of "steady state" situation for academic personnel.

During the years of the late 1960s and early 1970s, when the general trend was to curtail recruitment, the Department—again, along with the rest of the campus and along with many other institutions—began experiencing political pressures from both without and within to invoke affirmative action criteria in the hiring of faculty and other personnel. The sources of this pressure were diverse. It emanated most visibly from policies adopted by agencies of the federal government—particularly the Office of Health, Education, and Welfare—which pressed toward increased recruitment of minorities and women and which threatened to restrict federal research funds if evidence of such efforts to recruit was not forthcoming. Affirmative

8. Of new appointments made at the tenure level, Berkeley's department experienced a net gain of seven between 1952 and 1964 (seven new appointments, no resignations). Between 1964 and 1975, it experienced a net loss of three (four appointments, seven resignations).

action pressure also emanated from organized groups of minorities and women on the Berkeley campus, from faculty members in the Department who subscribed to the goals of affirmative action, and from organized political groups in the Bay Area.

Departmental hiring decisions reflected these pressures. Between 1948 and 1968 only one member of a group designated as "minority" (in this case a Japanese-American) was appointed as an assistant professor but was not promoted to tenure; no women were appointed in those years. As of the summer of 1969, the regular faculty was entirely non-minority and male. Between that time and 1974–75 nine new appointments to the regular faculty were made; of those, three were women, three were black males, and one was a Mexican American male. Minorities and women became more heavily represented among the temporary appointments as well. In addition to occasioning this change in pattern of initial appointments, affirmative-action considerations constituted the basis for additional conflict within the ranks of the faculty. Some members adhered doggedly to the application of traditional meritocratic standards in faculty recruitment and graduate student admission, and opposed the application of any special criteria that would increase the proportions of minorities and women. Others strongly urged the direct and aggressive application of such criteria. The majority of the faculty members tended to occupy some uneasy and unresolved compromise position between these two poles. On at least one occasion, conflict over an "incident" flared. In 1972–73 the Department was accused of having made a prior commitment to a white male candidate for appointment to a position of assistant professor, and thereby denying consideration to a qualified female candidate. That accusation generated some heat on the campus and among some members of the American Sociological Association. Ultimately the controversy spawned an investigation and report by a joint committee of the Pacific Sociological Association and the American Sociological Association, though no personnel actions on the part of the Department were altered as a result of that investigation.[9]

In sharp contrast to the dramatic shifts in volume and pattern of recruitment over the period of slightly more than two decades that we have just described, the *procedures* relied upon for recruitment constitute a model of invariance. Though some minor alterations in procedure could be traced from year to year, the following arrangements were typical throughout the period. Early in the academic year, perhaps in October, the Chairman of the Department would appoint one faculty member—always a tenured member and almost always a senior full professor—as Chairman of the Personnel Committee. In addition, he would appoint himself and two or three additional faculty members as members of that committee. The committee would be apprised by the Chairman—who in turn would have been apprised by the relevant Dean in the College of Letters and Science—as to the number and kinds of appointments that the Department might be expected to make and have approved during the coming academic year.

With respect to the appointment of junior faculty members, the Personnel Committee would initiate a search of a sort. This consisted mainly and sometimes entirely of commissioning members of the committee to write letters to colleagues and acquaintances in perhaps ten or fifteen graduate departments of sociology, informing them of the Department's intention to appoint, and asking for names of graduate students nearing completion of their dissertation who, in their estimation, were the most promising as scholars in the discipline. Letter writing was allocated to the committee members according to who knew whom best in what other institutions. Normally the positions

9. ASA *Footnotes* (August 1975), pp. 19–20.

were not advertised publicly. After the names of a number of outstanding graduate students had accumulated, the chairman of the Personnel Committee would write or sometimes telephone to secure various types of information from and about each candidate—graduate term papers, portions of a dissertation, written publications if any, and letters of reference from a few of the candidate's professors. No particular effort would be made to rank the candidates systematically according to explicit criteria; rather, members of the Personnel Committee would read the relevant materials and then attempt to reach consensus on which of the accumulated candidates were "best." Sometimes, though not typically, one or more candidates came to Berkeley for an interview. After a period of deliberation, the Personnel Committee prepared recommendations to be presented to the tenured faculty. In most cases the faculty would vote positively for the recommendation of the Personnel Committee. The recommended candidates would then be notified of the Department's action and asked whether they would be willing to accept an appointment. If so, the Chairman of the Department would prepare a recommendation to the Dean of the College of Letters and Science, a recommendation which was approved after review in all cases.

In the case of new appointments at the tenured level, the recruitment process was even more informal and unbureaucratic. In most cases the names of candidates were generated by informal discussions among members of the Personnel Committee and other Department members. Sometimes these discussions were supplemented by several letters or phone calls to senior scholars around the country, asking who were considered to be the most outstanding persons in a given area—in urban sociology, for example. Information would also be sought as to the possibility that some leading candidate might be pried away from his home institution. After departmental discussion produced a consensus or at least an overwhelming majority in favor

of a given candidate, that candidate would be contacted
and invited to pay a visit to Berkeley. The purpose of that
visit would typically not be to "look over" the candidate
but rather to persuade him to accept a forthcoming appointment. If that effort was successful, the Department
Chairman then prepared a "case" for the Dean for review
and approval by the administration.

Such procedures, though varying somewhat from year to
year and from one instance of recruitment to another, were
marked by informality, incompleteness of search, and lack
of systematic organization. While the Personnel Committee and the Department maintained a continuous commitment to what they regarded as the highest academic and
scientific standards, the precise nature of those
standards—as well as the precise way in which they were
applied to a given set of candidates—often remained implicit. In addition, information was gathered and influence
was sought in an informal network of scholars that was
constituted mainly by pooling the sociometric ties of the
members of any given year's Personnel Committee and
perhaps several other senior members of the Department.
Such procedures provided an adequate mechanism for
selecting high quality professional sociologists from a limited sample of elite institutions of graduate training. As a
search procedure, however, it did not cast a wide net.
Large numbers of graduate training institutions were never
contacted, and in all likelihood only a tiny minority of
potential candidates heard about the opening. Whatever
historical judgment we shall ultimately pass on such procedures, it must be noted that they held on with great
tenacity through the 1950s and 1960s, and into the early
1970s.

One final feature of those procedures should be noted:
their notably small requirements for supporting resources.
Normally the Department Chairman lent a portion of his
secretary's time to the Chairman of the Personnel Committee, who asked her to secure various kinds of information,

handle correspondence, and maintain a file for each active candidate. No office "hardware," beyond an electric type-writer, desks, filing cabinets, and a phone for long-distance calling, was required. Faculty evaluation time was, in effect, "costless," in the sense that service on the Personnel Committee was defined as one of the chores that any faculty member should be willing to take on periodi-cally; moreover, given the informality of the recruitment procedures, the demands on faculty time for evaluating candidates were hardly severe. The system was, in a word, very inexpensive.

1974–75: NEW REALITIES, OLD METHODS

We may consider the unsuccessful recruiting experience of the academic year 1974–75 as dramatic evidence of the fact that economic and political realities had generated a qualitatively new market situation, but at the same time the mechanism for recruitment and appointment had hardly changed. The fact of scarcity of new positions had been evident for a number of years. The Department had been granted one new appointment to be made in 1972–73, and one in 1973–74. The latter, an assistant professor in the area of Chicano studies, was the culmination of a long effort on the part of the Department to live up to its avowed commitment to appoint a scholar in that area. Scarcity endured into the 1974–75 year as well, as the Department was given only one position, in order to re-place a senior scholar who had resigned in 1973–74 to take a position in another university.

The fact of affirmative action was also much in evidence. Any position that was to be filled had to be advertised nationally in a professional sociological publication that would circulate widely several months before the actual appointment was made. The language of the advertisement had to be approved by the Berkeley campus' central admin-istration, and had to carry appropriate affirmative-action language. Given the increasing tightness of the academic market for sociologists at the time, such an advertisement, along with other publicity, was bound to generate between fifty and one hundred applicants for the position. In addition — also as a part of affirmative-action procedures — the Department was obliged to supply vast amounts of information to the administration about its search. This information included a description of the evaluation procedures used for all candidates, a listing of relevant background information on each (including ethnic membership and sex), and a statement of reasons why each unsuccessful applicant was not hired for the position. Such information was reviewed, moreover, by officials of the College of Letters and Science and by the campus affirmative-action office; if it was judged to be incomplete or otherwise unsatisfactory, it was returned to the Department for augmentation or other revision.

Clearly, then, the new environment for recruitment called for a level of publicity, comprehensiveness, and systematization that was unknown in the past. Yet on the side of procedure we retained a sort of "business-as-usual" posture. Smelser had just begun his term as Chairman of the Department. In accordance with custom, he appointed a five-person Personnel Committee, of which he was a member. The position was duly advertised in the American Sociological Association's publication *Footnotes,* and various members of the Personnel Committee wrote to colleagues around the country for nominations. As in the past, the Chairman agreed that part of his own secretary's duties would be to carry out the correspondence and maintain the files necessary for the search.

The subsequent search was a failure in three senses: first, the Personnel Committee and the Department could not make up their minds about what they were searching for; second, and partly though not totally the result of the first, it was difficult to keep the search moving; and third, the Department was unable to produce a single candidate for whom the Personnel Committee could develop consensus or enthusiasm. From the beginning, the search had an air of uncertainty about it. The senior faculty member who had departed was a person with strengths in research methods and mathematical sociology. Accordingly, in a Department meeting in October of 1974, it was agreed that the new appointee should have similar qualifications. Yet at that meeting some of the more "scientifically" inclined Department members expressed the hope that the appointee should be *primarily* a quantitative methodologist, whereas others believed that while he or she should be qualified in quantitative methods and make use of them in research, the appointee should also be evaluated according to his or her potential for substantive sociological contributions. In the end a formula was adopted—that the appointee be qualified in quantitative methods and have some substantive sociological interests. The ambivalence developed over what kind of "methods person" we wanted carried over to the Personnel Committee. In consequence, with this vagueness of charge, members of that committee forever tended to ask of any candidate, "Is this the *kind* of candidate we want, or should we be looking for some other kind?"

There was a second note of ambiguity as well. Because the new appointment was defined as a "replacement" for the departed senior scholar, and some Department members believed that it would be difficult to recruit a really good junior person in the area of quantitative methods, the hope was expressed that the Department should be permitted to hire at the senior level if that seemed desirable. Smelser approached the Dean and secured approval to recommend an appointee without regard to rank, though it was understood that if a senior person were recommended, a very special series of arguments would have to be advanced to bolster the case for such an appointment. Again, the uncertainty with respect to rank carried over into the search; members of the Personnel Committee never sorted out in their own minds the importance they should assign to rank, and, correspondingly, the search for both senior and junior candidates was somewhat halfhearted.

Perhaps these circumstances alone were sufficient to stall the search. Also contributing, we perceive, were a certain casualness and informality in the Personnel Committee's way of proceeding, on the one hand, and what turned out to be a woeful inadequacy of resources on the other. The committee set no deadlines for completing the preliminary screening of the mass of candidates who applied, for narrowing the list to a manageable number of outstanding or promising candidates, for bringing candidates to Berkeley for interviews, or for reaching a final decision. Following its customary review procedures of passing bundles of files on candidates from faculty member to faculty member, the Committee found itself burdened with too many files to evaluate thoroughly and promptly, and found itself continuously falling behind. On the non-academic side, the situation was even more desperate. The Chairman's secretary was overwhelmed with a flood of applications, curricula vitae, letters of reference, and written materials of candidates, almost all of which required acknowledgment and further correspondence. She, like the Personnel Committee, found herself continuously falling behind in the accumulation of materials in the files.

At a certain despondent moment in the spring of 1975, Smelser concluded that there was no real possibility of producing a candidate whom we could recommend with positive enthusiasm to the Department or the campus administration. He approached the Dean, requested permission *not* to have to fill the position, and secured a pledge that the vacancy would be held open for the Department for the following year.

CHAPTER 5

Devising a Rational
Recruitment Plan

THE DEPARTMENT SCENE, 1975–76

The unsuccessful search for a single appointee in 1974–75
left a number of us with feelings of frustration and disap-
pointment. Some of us feared that the Department was so
divided on so many issues that it might not be possible to
secure a sufficiently enthusiastic response to *any* candidate
to permit us to make a strong case to the administration
for his or her appointment, or to permit that candidate to
feel welcome among prospective colleagues. At the same
time, the summer of 1975 brought to the Department an
opportunity for recruitment the abundance of which could
scarcely be imagined in the mid-1970s. Such an opportunity called for an ambitious recruiting campaign on the
Department's part; but it was equally apparent that without new and reorganized resources we could not mount
such a campaign. In this chapter we shall first develop a
more elaborated statement of these opportunities and obstacles. Then we shall report on the plan of action we
developed and believed to be rational.

The New Positions

As a result of a series of unconnected circumstances, the
Department found itself with a number of vacancies occurring in 1975–76—vacancies which, if not filled in a

77

reasonable time, would seriously impair the Department's
ability to offer adequate teaching programs at the graduate
and undergraduate levels. The first vacancy was the
"methods slot" which opened when our senior colleague
departed, and which was left unfilled in 1974–75. Two
more vacancies occurred as a result of the non-promotion of
two assistant professors, one effective in the summer of
1975 and the other in the summer of 1976. And finally,
two retirements were scheduled to occur in the summer of
1976. Between 1974 and 1976, then, the Department was
scheduled to lose almost 20 percent of its members.

   In 1974, at the request of the Provost of the College of
Letters and Science, Smelser had prepared a statement of a
five-year academic plan for the Department. Anticipating
the probability of upcoming vacancies, he made an effort
to diagnose the strengths and weaknesses of the Department and to develop a statement of future needs on the
basis of that diagnosis. Smelser characterized the Department as very strong in social theory, historical and comparative institutional analysis (with some points of inadequacy, however), and social psychology. He argued
further that as a result of the Department's current
composition—as well as its anticipated composition in the
wake of the five vacancies—it had or promised to develop
weaknesses in the areas of demography, urban sociology,
social stratification, and quantitative methods. Following
on this assessment, he argued that in order to maintain its
strength, the Department would require *six* new regular
faculty positions over the coming two-year period.

   In the spring of 1975, Smelser was given informal
assurance that the department would be allocated three
positions to be filled at the assistant professor level during
the academic year 1975–76. The Dean agreed with
Smelser's reasoning and request but explicitly limited the
Department to three positions for one year on the grounds
that it did not have sufficient resources to conduct a search
for additional appointees. The Dean also indicated, infor-

mally, that two or three more positions would probably become available to be filled during 1976–77.

One problem we encountered immediately was that of timing. Although the Dean could give informal guarantees of the three positions, actual campus approval had to await a long period of review, negotiating, and infighting at higher administrative levels. Final approval of the positions was not expected until sometime in November 1975. That was a source of alarm; if we had to wait until final approval of the positions to begin our search, we would already be well into the recruiting season, and it would not be possible to mobilize Departmental energies to conduct a proper search. Smelser requested permission to advertise the positions and move into the initial phases of a search in the summer of 1975, even though the positions were still "soft." The Dean acquiesced, but insisted that we protect ourselves by indicating in advertisements and other communications that the positions were only "anticipated."

A second problem involved the designation of the positions. Both Smelser and the Dean agreed that the positions should be described in a way that was consistent with the recommendations of the five-year academic plan. The major problem was: how precisely to designate the positions? Smelser was inclined to describe them in as general terms as possible, in order to give the department maximum flexibility in considering the greatest number of candidates. On the other hand, affirmative action considerations demanded that the Department specify the positions in rather concise terms. (The rationale was that clarity of specification diminishes the possibility that candidates could be excluded arbitrarily on grounds that they do not fit vaguely designated areas.) After a certain amount of negotiation the following formulation was accepted:

1. One appointment of an assistant professor in the area of quantitative research methods, but without specification with respect to substantive sociological interests. This position was, in effect, a description of the unfilled position

from the previous year. The Dean left open the remotest possibility that he would entertain a recommendation for a senior position, but strongly discouraged the Department from thinking about senior people in methods.

2. One appointment of an assistant professor in comparative sociology. The Department was especially interested in candidates who had background in comparative research relating to China, Africa, or Latin America, where it was weak. We agreed, however, that the Department was not *bound* to recruit someone with special interests in one of those three areas. A further justification for asking for this position was that one of the non-promoted assistant professors and one of the retiring professors were comparative sociologists.

3. One appointment of an assistant professor in the area of demography, stratification, or urban sociology, or some combination of these related sub-fields. This position was something of a residual, and gave the Department considerable latitude. Part of the justification for this position was that one of the retiring faculty members was especially strong in demography and urban sociology.

Departmental Divisions and the Difficulty of Generating Consensus

The "atmosphere" of an academic department is an exceptionally elusive phenomenon: it is invariably complex; it is so intangible as to defy its own characterization; and when characterization is attempted, different perceptions and disagreements emerge. Despite these difficulties, we must try our hands at such a description, since that atmosphere proved to be a fundamental dimension to be taken into account when seeking agreement on who one's future colleagues are to be.

As of the early 1970s—and extending back into the turbulent days of the 1960s—the Berkeley sociology faculty found it difficult to secure consensus on many issues it faced, because of a number of conflicting perspectives and corresponding political divisions. We believe that such cleavages are probably typical in academic departments; we imagine further that they are likely to be severe in a discipline like sociology, which is "multi-paradigmatic" in character and which has attained only partial legitimacy as a scientific field of learning. While we have not surveyed other academic departments in sociology, moreover, it is our impression that the Berkeley Department ranked above average in measures of diversity of substantive interests, styles of scholarship, and ideological commitments—to say nothing of the loyalties and antagonisms that inevitably accompany these types of diversity. What underlay this pervasive tendency toward divisiveness and the corresponding difficulty in securing consensus? We do not know; but we believe it possible to specify some of the overlapping but at the same time crisscrossing fault lines—which, when juxtaposed, made for a propensity to polarize. The following lines of division seem to be the most salient:

Substantive areas of sociological interest and work. Each individual faculty member had, during the course of his or her scholarly work, developed interests in and a claim over substantive areas of sociology—sociology of the family, urban sociology, social psychology of various sorts, demography, political sociology, and so on. In varying degrees and at varying times, a faculty member would assume a defensive or aggrandizing posture towards his or her area of specialization. By and large, in terms of the addition of new academic personnel, different individuals in the Department would be inclined to favor appointments in substantive areas in which they themselves were committed and accomplished. This "jurisdictional" approach to recruitment was, however, tempered by a genuine commitment on the part of many faculty members to strive for an encompassing, balanced representation of substantive sociological interests in the Department.

Different sociological styles. Again, this is more nearly a map than a dimension. The Department contained traditional scholars who labored over historical archives in the libraries, individuals whose mode was the quantitative analysis of survey or demographic data, those who analyzed institutional data on a comparative basis, and those who relied on rich ethnographic descriptions based on participant observation in field situations. As in the case of the commitments to different substantive areas of sociology, individual faculty members tended to favor their own over others' styles, though many were also committed to a posture of catholicity with respect to sociological style.

Difference in sociological "schools." The Berkeley department was sufficiently large and diverse to include an ample representation of functionalists, conflict theorists, radical or neo-Marxist theorists of various stripes, symbolic interactionists, and empirical researchers of eclectic theoretical persuasion. Representatives of those diverse approaches embraced their own and criticized others with varying degrees of passion; but these potential bases of conflict were also softened by an ideology of tolerance that characterized many faculty members' outlooks.

In any Departmental meeting or discussion, these potential bases for division were inevitably in the wings, and would emerge from time to time. Overlaying these differences, moreover, were several additional divisions, with respect to which passions often seemed to run deeper.

Emphasis on "scientific standards" in sociology versus some version of "humanistic" sociology. On the one side of this division is a persistent emphasis on giving priority in sociological research to the observation of scientific norms at both the theoretical and methodological levels. Adherents to the "scientific" standards end of the dimension were more likely to be committed to mathematical models, quantitative statistical techniques, and rigorous research design. They were not committed to the investigation of any particular kind of subject matter. They were also inclined to regard those committed to the "humanistic" side as "soft." "Humanistic" sociologists had different substantive and methodological preoccupations. In particular, they tended to select for study and commentary various kinds of social phenomena that inevitably involve inequality and disadvantage—phenomena such as poverty, crime, deviance, and exploitation and oppression generally. Those adhering to this emphasis tended to identify with the disadvantaged, and tended to stress the human costs that are exacted from them by contemporary social arrangements. They laid less emphasis on strict adherence to scientific norms, and regarded those who did as rigid, unimaginative, unconcerned, and conservative. In characterizing this dimension we have had to oversimplify and do certain violence to many subtle differences in individuals' outlooks. We should also point out that this particular basis for division was also softened by a shared commitment to canons of representing and evaluating data as adequately as possible and gearing general inferences to what was revealed in available data.

Positions taken on past political issues. Sociologists, perhaps more than many other social scientists, became deeply involved in the turbulences of the 1960s and early 1970s—civil rights, anti-war activity, women's liberation, and the student assault on university authority. Their concern and involvement, however, did not produce agreement on either the diagnosis or the evaluation of those turbulences. The Department experienced numerous crises in the 1960s, when it was called upon to take some kind of public stand on issues of extreme political importance, such as the American incursion into Cambodia in the spring of 1970. Invariably, such a crisis resulted in a deep division. Those issues were no longer salient in 1975, but the cleavages that had crystallized in the years of turbulence had established complex patterns of loyalty and distrust that had persisted. Those past divisions often lingered in later debates and in votes on seemingly unrelated academic issues.

Attitudes toward graduate students. At one end of this dimension is a complex of attitudes that includes a commitment to maintain faculty authority in curricular design and execution, to insist on rigorous standards of performance in evaluating graduate students, to restrict graduate student participation in departmental affairs, and generally to be negatively influenced by political and academic stances taken by graduate student organizations. At the other end are the opposite orientations: to maintain more nearly equal relations with graduate students, to place less stress on evaluations according to rigorous standards, to afford maximum freedom to graduate students in pursuing their studies, to encourage graduate involvement in departmental business, and to be more positively swayed by expressions of graduate student sentiment.

Emphasis on "standards" versus "affirmative action." This dimension requires little amplification; it involves a conflict between the application of traditional criteria of academic excellence and the application of alternative criteria (such as relevant non-academic experience), as well as past disadvantage, in admission to graduate study, recruitment, and promotion.

Although these various bases for division did not coincide with one another precisely, and it was not possible to place any individual faculty member consistently on the dimensions, the Department members tended to line up more or less consistently, no matter what issue was under consideration—the promotion of an assistant professor, the recruitment of a new faculty member, the degree to which course sequences in research methods should be required of graduate students, the degree of structure or rigor to be incorporated into the undergraduate curriculum, or admission policies. Even on those issues on which it was eventually possible to gain more or less unanimous votes, these divisions were in evidence, expressing themselves perhaps in a vigorous debate on some critical amendment prior to final action on the main issue, or perhaps in varying degrees of lukewarmness toward a generally acceptable policy. On any given issue it could be safely anticipated that four or five—perhaps a few more—department members would consistently adopt a "left" orientation (including a vague admixture of "humanistic," politically left, pro-graduate student, affirmative-action elements, depending on the issue at hand), and that a like number would adopt a "right" orientation (including the opposing ingredients). Typically, also, perhaps a dozen faculty members would array themselves in varying stances in the middle, generally attempting to seek compromise formulations and solutions, often splitting, but generally holding a precarious balance of influence.

We believe this characterization of the Departmental atmosphere to be more or less accurate, though others would probably give different renditions. (Indeed, it is the nature of the particular divisions we have described that different participants will give different and conflicting versions of the nature of Departmental reality.) Even if only approximate, however, it suggests the delicate navigation that would be required to secure Departmental consensus on the appointment of several new assistant professors.

Limited Resources for Recruitment

The unhappy search of 1974–75 had revealed, among other things, the severely limited staff and financial resources available to conduct a search for even one appointee in the existing market situation. With the prospect of appointing three new faculty members, the limitations became much more evident. Indeed, it was the Dean's awareness of those limitations that led him to restrict the number of appointments to three, even though a case could be made for a larger number, given current losses. Faculty resources themselves were limited. As indicated earlier, the Department was not especially large, and only a limited amount of faculty time could be devoted to personnel recruitment, given the multiplicity of other demands on its members. The situation was even graver on the side of the non-academic staff. Even if she had been assigned full-time to the task of maintaining personnel files, correspondence, and other essential recruiting activities, the Chairman's secretary would have been overwhelmed. Furthermore, given the primitive office technology, it appeared that the addition of enough new non-academic staff members would have to be so great as to disrupt other activities of the Departmental office, such as graduate admissions and undergraduate advising. Finally, the Department had no budgeted funds to cover the direct costs of the search—the costs of advertising the position and, more important, of transporting finalist candidates to Berkeley from around the country for personal interviews and presentation of scholarly materials. The Department's regular budget could probably absorb some of the additional costs, such as increased mailing, duplication, and telephone costs, but these constituted only a fraction of the total required.

DESIGNING THE NEW SEARCH

The general picture in the summer of 1975, then, was one of considerable opportunity and challenge, within a somewhat uncertain and inauspicious setting. In those months, Smelser and Content gradually developed three convictions in their own minds: that the search for new faculty was by far the most important departmental priority for 1975–76; that that search had to take into account the new conditions in the academic marketplace, especially the existence of a buyer's market and of affirmative-action policies; and that the search would have no chance of success unless a major reorganization of departmental resources was effected and additional extra-departmental resources were secured. Guided by these convictions, we devoted most of our effort that summer to designing and carrying out the initial phases of the most rational plan we could conceive. We describe that plan now, in a way more or less identical to the way we developed it then—that is to say, in pure form; we shall reserve until the next chapter the account of the diversions, alterations, and adaptations that unfolded as we attempted to execute the plan in the ensuing months.

The Goals

Basing our reasoning on as careful a diagnosis of the Departmental and external situation as we could, we formulated the following goals around which to organize the search. These goals, with the legitimizing consideration for each, were the following:

1. The recruitment program should generate the largest possible pool of candidates for each position. (Here we were concerned with the criterion of academic excellence, or turning up the widest array of talent; and with the criterion of affirmative action, or not bypassing the less conspicuous corners of the market, where promising minority and female candidates might be located.)

2. All candidates should receive a consistent, careful, and thorough consideration of their qualifications and potential for appointment to a faculty position in the Department, and exact records should be kept of all factors leading to eventual selection or rejection for such a position.[1] (Here we are concerned with three sets of criteria:

1. As we shall see, this insistence on the consistent application of manifestly identical criteria in the assessment of candidates was to have an ultimate political significance as well, though we did not formulate that goal with political considerations explicitly in mind. See Chapter Six.

first, academic excellence, or developing a systematic series of standards of assessment; equity, or assuring all candidates of equally systematic evaluation; and affirmative action, or detailing the procedures by which all candidates would be evaluated and the considerations that would ultimately lead to the recommendation of some and the rejection of others.)

3. The major effort required for an effective search for new faculty should not seriously disrupt the department's other responsibilities for undergraduate teaching and advising, graduate training, placement of graduate students, review of current academic and staff personnel, and all support activities associated with these activities. (Here the rationale was simply to assure administrative continuity during the period of the search.)

4. A subsequent analysis of the year's recruitment activity should be undertaken. (The rationale here was simply that we wished to increase our information about recruitment and hopefully provide recommendations for future efforts.)

To implement these goals, we began to undertake a number of concrete steps.

Publicizing the Position

In order to cast the widest possible net for young sociological talent in the nation, we decided on two forms of public advertisement. First, we listed the vacancies with the placement service of the American Sociological Association, which was a feature of the meetings of the ASA scheduled for late August 1975 in San Francisco. Smelser and Content planned to make themselves available at those meetings to interview potential candidates and answer questions they might have about the search and the Department. Second, we placed an advertisement in the American Sociological Association's official publication, *Footnotes,* which was mailed to every member of the Association on a regular basis (see Appendix A for the advertisement).[2] To supplement this publicity, Smelser wrote letters of inquiry to chairpersons of approximately forty departments with graduate training programs around the country, describing the positions in the language of the advertisement and requesting the names of their most promising graduate students who might be appropriate candidates for one or more of the positions. Smelser also wrote—and invited a number of Berkeley colleagues to write—similar letters to known professional colleagues around the country; approximately one hundred such letters were sent. Finally, we decided to include categories of unsolicited applicants among our active candidates. The first category would consist of those persons recommended by faculty members involved in graduate training who took the initiative in attempting to place their outstanding students; this group of colleagues hopefully would bring to our attention some candidates not uncovered by our own initiative. The second category would consist of applications from individuals who apparently had not used any of the other sources.

In publicizing the position, we made an effort to record which of the several recruitment sources was being used by each candidate. This mechanism consisted of varying our Department's address in minor detail. For example, we asked chairmen to make their referrals to Smelser at Box C, Department of Sociology, University of California, Berkeley, California 94720. In the *Footnotes* advertisement we instructed applicants to write to the same address, but to Box F. We approached some of the additional labels in a somewhat lighter spirit. We requested those one hundred known professional colleagues to respond to Smelser at Box B (short for "buddy").[3] We decided to code those applicants who appeared at the placement service at the ASA

2. Placing this advertisement was simultaneously a decision on our part and an act of conformity with one of the requirements associated with the campus's affirmative-action policies.

3. Apparently some of these instructions found their way into the address books and files of professional colleagues. A certain proportion of Smelser's professional mail is still addressed to "Box C" or "Box B."

meetings as "Box S" (for "slave market"). And for those few students from our own department at Berkeley who expressed an interest in one of the positions, we generated a special "Box I" (for "inbreeding" or "incest"). To the extent that our instructions for identifying a box number were followed, it was possible for purposes of subsequent analysis to determine what recruitment sources were effective in generating candidates—and, more important, in generating what different kinds of candidates. We shall report some results of these analyses in Chapter Seven.

Informing the Faculty

In late September 1975, Smelser called a faculty meeting devoted exclusively to recruitment of academic personnel for the coming year. He explained what had happened already with respect to authorizing, describing, and advertising the positions, and what organizational changes in recruitment were going to be implemented. He stressed the fundamental importance of the search for the Department's future, indicating that in the next two years the faculty would be experiencing a turnover of between 20 and 25 percent, and that the long-range academic future of the department depended upon the care and excellence with which we conducted our academic search and appointment process. He also stressed the necessity of filling the positions, reminding the faculty that we had not filled a position the preceding year, and that if we did not fill those three positions the administration might allocate them elsewhere in the College. While not designed as such at that time, that message now appears as the first effort in Smelser's campaign to influence the faculty to come to some sort of acceptable consensus: an effort to invoke an outside administrative threat as a means to prod the faculty into more or less concerted action.[4] In fact, he exaggerated

4. One year earlier, in the fall of 1974, the Department undertook to reorganize its undergraduate major curriculum, after a College-wide review and after pressure was applied from the Office of the Provost and Dean. At that

the threat: the Dean had, indeed, strongly expressed the hope that the department would fill the positions, but he had not actually threatened to withdraw them.

Involving the Faculty in the Search

In the course of designing the new procedures, Smelser concluded early in the summer of 1975 that the time-honored method of a single personnel committee to evaluate applicants and recommend them to the Department would not suffice for the coming year's search. On grounds of workload alone, such an arrangement seemed archaic; we anticipated between fifty and one hundred applicants for each position, and a committee of five would soon be either buried under paper or would be forced to begin cutting corners by giving hasty reviews to many of the applicants. Also, since the range of positions to be filled was quite wide—involving, it will be recalled, one position in quantitative methods, one in comparative sociology, and one in demography-urban-stratification—a committee of five would have to spread itself thin substantively while reviewing all candidates in all three areas; it seemed advisable to bring more faculty expertise to bear in the initial evaluation process. At the same time, it seemed advisable to continue the practice of having a *group* of faculty members present recommendations to the department for full discussion and final vote.

Keeping these considerations in mind, Smelser decided to continue the practice of having one central personnel committee responsible for formulating final recommendations to the faculty as a whole. In picking this committee of five, he kept a number of criteria in mind.

---

time, too, there was a kind of conditional threat that the Sociology Department could not expect continuing support from the administration if it did not reform its undergraduate major. That outside threat provided, in our estimation, the effective pressure for the faculty to formulate and adopt a new policy in an academic area in which it was, in fact, deeply divided on grounds of curricular philosophy.

Insofar as possible, it should be staffed with conscientious faculty members, willing to complete the work of evaluation reasonably promptly and willing to observe disciplined judgments in their evaluations. Yet at the same time the committee, if its recommendations were to carry force, itself had to be representative of a wide range of departmental interests, styles, and political divisions. It should have minority and women representatives; it should, insofar as possible, have a member who bore the trust of and who could communicate freely with the major groupings in the department. If it did not have these ingredients, its own credibility would have been limited, along with its usefulness as a consensus-forming mechanism.

At the same time, the personnel committee was expanded according to a definitive principle. Three of its members were designated as chairpersons of three special subcommittees, each corresponding to one of the three positions advertised. The membership of each of these subcommittees was completed by appointing two or three *additional* faculty members, chosen on the basis of their interests and qualification for reviewing candidates in the respective areas of specialization. This yielded the following committee structure:

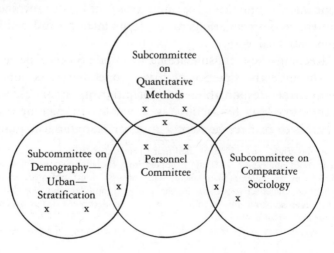

Each subcommittee was assigned all the files of the applicants in its area, and was encouraged to expand the pool of candidates, on its own, in any way it believed appropriate (for example, by telephoning additional colleagues in other institutions). Instead of preparing the results of its evaluations as a recommendation to the entire department, however, each subcommittee was to submit them to the personnel committee as a whole, who would review them and make the final presentation to the departmental faculty.

The initial assignment of candidates to the various subcommittees was made by Smelser's staff, independently in obvious cases, in consultation with him in ambiguous ones. Then the files were given to a number of individual faculty members for independent evaluations. These evaluations were pooled and made collective first at the subcommittee level, next at the level of the personnel committee, and finally at the level of the faculty as a whole. This process, contrived in the first instance as a mechanism to increase faculty resources and facilitate the work flow, had in the end an unanticipated consensus-building consequence. As a result of expanding the procedures in this way, almost half the faculty became involved in the reviewing process from the beginning, which helped avoid the negative reaction that sometimes occurs when a small committee "springs" what appears to be a final recommendation on a much larger departmental faculty which has not been involved in the processes that led up to that recommendation. In addition, the expanded faculty participation meant that for any given candidate who might be recommended to the faculty as a whole, at least seven faculty members would have been involved in the process of building that recommendation, even though all of them may not have personally agreed with it.

Establishing Evaluation Procedures

To systematize and standardize the evaluation procedures, we instituted a common series of practices. These were designed to approach—however imperfectly—the ideal of securing identical types of materials from each candidate and subjecting that information to review under categories of assessment that were also identical or very similar. To that end, we asked every candidate—once he or she was judged to be "active"—to submit a standard curriculum vitae, at least one sample of published or unpublished written work, and the names of at least three persons who could supply letters of recommendation. Once the files contained this information—plus the three or more letters of reference—it was judged to be "circulable" and given in sequence to each member of the relevant committee. Each evaluator was asked to rank the candidate with regard to his or her potential for excellence in a faculty position at Berkeley. Rather than rely on global judgments of excellence by individuals, which might be based on various unknown and idiosyncratic criteria, we attempted to establish two precautions:

1. We asked that the file of each candidate be reviewed by at least three faculty members independently—that is, with no evaluator having any prior knowledge of any other evaluator's assessments.

2. We asked that each evaluator, rather than giving an overall ranking of candidates with the relative weighting of factors unclear, provide three separate rankings of each candidate's potential: (a) career to date (for example, record of academic excellence, teaching experience, professional commitment); (b) written work (paying attention to such issues as quality, quantity, single or multiple authorship); (c) letters of recommendation (paying attention to both the strength of the recommendation and the reputation of the recommenders for candid evaluations).

As one final guide for the faculty evaluators, Smelser prepared a list of questions to be kept in mind for each of the three types of ranking (see Appendix B). While acknowledging that evaluators would attend to these guidelines with varying degrees of conscientiousness, we felt it was a move in the direction of assuring that applicants would receive more detailed consideration, and that it guarded against the likelihood of a candidate being dropped from consideration because of some anomaly in his or her record.

Involving Graduate Students in the Search

Given the stormy history of the relations between graduate students and faculty, the problem of involving graduate students appropriately—if at all—in the search process proved to be a delicate one. Up to that time, students' evaluations of new appointees and faculty members being considered for promotion had been gathered on an informal basis, with recommendations being submitted by groups of students and evaluations being sought from students who had worked closely with the faculty member. On occasion, students would take the initiative and express support for a faculty member at the time he or she was being evaluated for tenure.

In the fall of 1975, representatives of the Graduate Student Union—the official organization of graduate students in the Department—approached Smelser and requested some sort of involvement in the search and recommendation procedures. After extensive discussions with the personnel committee and negotiations with students, it was possible to work out a limited form of participation of graduate students. Selected graduate students were to be called up to provide supplementary evaluations of candidates' written work and vitae; they were persuaded, however, that letters of recommendation about the candidates—who might be future teachers of the graduate students—be withheld from graduate student review. Later in the review process, groups of students were asked to prepare written reports on candidates after their visits to Berkeley, during which they would make formal presentations and would be interviewed by groups of graduate students. Such reports by graduate students were to be regarded as advisory, with final recommendations for the appointment of the candidates remaining with the faculty.

Reorganizing the Non-academic Staff

As indicated, one of the most vulnerable parts of the search procedure was the lack of non-academic staff support for the search. In the summer of 1975, Smelser and Content moved to improve that support and to secure improved technological equipment to facilitate disposing of the mountain of clerical details that would be part of the expanded search. As for the staff itself, we transferred Smelser's secretary to the role of full-time faculty secretary, and appropriated a portion of the time of another staff member to serve as his part-time secretary. Content moved into a room adjacent to Smelser's office and took primary and direct responsibility for staff coordination of the search. In addition, the undergraduate secretary was relieved of some of her existing duties and assigned on a half-time basis to the personnel search process. These changes increased the proportion of staff time in the search, and moved the operation centrally into Smelser's office.

Using New Technological Aids

To assault the problem of the great anticipated volume of correspondence, we proposed to lease an automatic, magnetic-card typewriter to produce the basic (and basically repetitive) letters required in the recruitment process. This machine would make possible prompt attention to all necessary correspondence and assure that the recruitment effort would not invade and disrupt the many other typing activities required by Department business. In addition, the machine promised to be of service in graduate admissions, which also involved much repetitive correspondence, as well as in attempting to find employment for our own graduate students, an operation which was, by then, calling for a greater volume of letters of recommendation, as students hedged their bets by applying to many potential employers.

The second and more innovative way in which we attempted to increase efficiency was to make use of an interactive mini-computer to keep daily records of all recruitment activity. We discovered a computer program named PERSON, which had been developed by the Lawrence Hall of Science on the Berkeley campus, and which, with several modifications, promised to meet our basic requirements. The program we ultimately adopted, called RECRUIT, provided a convenient and accessible file system for tracking recruitment activity, as well as storage for data to be subsequently analyzed. Confidentiality and limited access to the storage file on the computer was provided through the use of a secret and frequently changed code entry. The file included an entry for every candidate under consideration. The first entry would be made at the time the candidate's name was received—regardless of recruitment source—and was extended and completed on a daily basis as additional information was generated. The basic elements of the file entries were as follows:

1. Name
2. Recruitment Source (the box code described above, being an elaboration of the information required by Form II of the Berkeley affirmative action guidelines)
3. Area of Candidate's Specialization (coded and ranked according to departmental priorities as expressed in its advertisements)
4. Sex
5. Ethnicity
6. Most Advanced Degree
7. Date of Degree

8. Institution of Degree
9. Zip Code (for subsequent geographical analysis of the candidate pool)
10. File Control Code (indicating status of the file—whether incomplete, circulating, circulated)
11. File Location Code (indicating where the file is—the pending drawer, Professor Smith, the complete drawer)
12. Evaluator's Rankings
    (a)   Career
    (b)   Written work
    (c)   References
13. Final Action (incorporating codes from Form II).

In addition to providing instant information on the status of any application, the RECRUIT program promised to generate ranked or alphabetical lists on any of the indices, or combinations thereof—for example, a list of women candidates whose specializations were within our priority fields of specialization. Once faculty evaluations were complete, moreover, it would be possible to generate lists of candidates from these rankings both on an individual criterion (such as written work), and on various combinations of unweighted or weighted criteria.

Securing Financial Support for the Search

Normally the annual budget for the Sociology Department, like all departments at Berkeley, is set in advance, and provides little flexibility for allocating funds from one category of expenditure to another. We discovered that we simply could not finance the new hardware from our own budget. In our plan, then, we had to anticipate a search for funding from outside the Department. We will give an account of that search in the next chapter.

Such was our plan, as of the late summer and early fall of 1975. It seemed to us well-laid, being based on our diagnosis of the Department's situation and environment and on our prognosis for the search and recruitment process. As with most plans of this sort, however, the execution corresponded only vaguely and uncertainly with the conception.

CHAPTER 6

The Rational Plan Confronts Reality

We will tell the story of the search and recruitment chronologically, beginning with the initial mailing of letters to chairpersons and colleagues in the summer of 1975, and ending with our negotiations with the handful of persons who emerged as our final choices from the nearly three hundred applicants who were considered during the search period. From time to time, however, we will break into the chronology and digress, in order to identify and discuss some special problems we confronted, or to analyze and speculate on some special facet of the search process.

CASTING THE INITIAL NET

After gaining permission from the campus administration to proceed, we reproduced some 140 letters on the magnetic-card typewriter, and sent them to chairpersons and colleagues throughout the country in July and August. Most of these were signed by Smelser as Department chairman, a number by the chairman of the personnel committee, and a scattering by other members of the personnel committee. The letters to chairpersons yielded a total of 31 candidates (of an ultimate total of 285), and the letters to professional colleagues yielded an additional 74 candidates. The latter figure constitutes the largest number from any single source (the placement service yielded 58 candidates and the advertisement in *Footnotes* brought 65, which suggests that the "network" of professional contacts continued to be a major source of potential recruits. It is difficult to place too much confidence in this judgment, however, since the letters were sought in the initial phase of the search, *before* the ASA convention and the placing of the advertisement, and it is impossible to know how many of those who were recommended in response to the letters might also have responded to one of the two public advertisements.[1] In any event, it proved possible to begin contacting a sizable number of candidates and their references at an early date for the necessary information and evaluations.

THE PLACEMENT SERVICE

We must confess that in considering the use of the professional placement service of the American Sociological Association, our existing image of that kind of service was mainly negative. Part of this stemmed from our perception that it was a kind of impersonal, crassly instrumental process, as conveyed by the term "slave market," which is often applied to it. In addition, recognizing the importance of other mechanisms, particularly collegial networks, we shared to some degree Caplow and McGee's view that "there is a tendency in most fields for only the weakest candidates to use the services of a placement agency."[2] We believed further that much of the activity would consist of last-minute searches on the part of both the unemployed and schools with unanticipated vacancies. Given this negative image and given our own limited financial resources, we probably would not have participated actively if the convention had been elsewhere than San Francisco, which was easily accessible to us by local public transportation.

1. As indicated, the letters were mailed in July and August of 1975; the dates of the ASA meetings were August 25–29; and the ad in *Footnotes,* while scheduled to appear in October, actually did not appear until the first days of November, because of a delay in the Executive Office of the ASA.

2. Theodore Caplow and Reece McGee, *The Academic Marketplace* (New York: Basic Books, 1958), p. 121.

Our experience with the service was to prove our expectations incorrect.

Matters began somewhat inauspiciously, for we discovered we could not find the actual location of the placement service. We finally came upon it in a hotel some distance from the main convention hotel site. That location seemed to symbolize the secondary position of the placement activities and promised to aggravate any communication problems we might have in contacting candidates. The placement routine was such that during the first two days of the meetings prospective employers and prospective candidates did not actually see one another; candidates had access to our listings and could indicate a desire to be interviewed later, and we had access to a massive book of one-page listings of candidates who had registered with the service. Discouraged by the large numbers of applicants and by the small amount of information on each, we decided to interview only those applicants who expressed an interest in our announcement. Despite this early lack of communication, the response to our listings was very strong, and before the convention was over, more than sixty "request for interview" slips had been placed in the Berkeley "box." (That number was larger than the ultimate number of applicants brought to our attention through the placement service, which was 58, because a few persons had expressed an interest in more than one of the three advertised positions.)

That initial response was the first tangible confirmation of how large an operation the ultimate search was going to be. In fact, we were unable to schedule interviews for all of the several dozen applicants, so we selected randomly from the list, scheduling 15-minute interviews with those selected, and instructing the remainder as to the appropriate procedures if they wished to formalize their applications. We also decided that, given the numbers of applicants, it would be absurd to attempt to "interview" each one in an evaluative sense; instead we used the brief meetings to establish contact, explain our planned selection procedures, collect any materials the candidate had available, and answer any questions about the procedures or the Berkeley Department.

The interviews themselves provided us with further clues of what we were to discover later. During the first morning of the interviewing, Smelser met and talked with ten candidates. Contrary to prior expectation, he was struck by the strength of many of the candidates and with the high proportion that seemed to come from leading graduate programs. He also was struck with their obviously high motivation and their evident desire to make a strong, positive impression. In fact, he asked Content after the end of the interviewing sessions if she had deliberately selected candidates for him who looked strong "on paper," and was told that they had been assigned on a completely random basis. This suggested that a certain amount of "self-selection" was occurring—that is, those taking the trouble to apply were primarily candidates who thought they might have a realistic chance to be hired at Berkeley (a chance based mainly on where they had received their training, how talented others—and themselves—had told them they were, and so on). Toward the end of the interviews Content asked several of the candidates about the possibility of self-selection, and they frankly acknowledged that they had observed groups of candidates discussing among themselves whether it would be worth their while placing themselves in our competition. Throughout the search we gained further confirmation that self-selection was a very powerful factor contributing to the ultimate composition of the total pool of applicants.[3]

As we shall indicate below, most of those who applied through the placement service did not end up on the final

3. For a breakdown of applicants according to institution of origin, see Chapter Seven.

list of candidates; for that matter, however, neither did most of those secured from any other source. It was notable, moreover, that two of the final four appointees were contacted initially through the placement service, and one of these exclusively there—that is to say, she did not turn up in our network of chairpersons and colleagues.[4]

Our experience at the placement service taught us early and forcefully, in short, that we were indeed in a buyer's market, and that we should expect an abundance of strength among our applicants.

THE EARLY MONTHS OF REVIEWING

The months of September through December were lacking in dramatic moments, but the amount of staff and faculty labor dedicated to the search process was enormous. On the staff side, it was a matter of writing hundreds, indeed thousands, of letters to candidates and referees—to request information, written materials, and evaluations, as well as acknowledging receipt of these materials. It was also a matter of painstakingly recording and entering all this information, on a day-by-day basis, into the computer. For each of the faculty members it meant many hours reading over dozens of files, deliberating, and entering the appropriate evaluations in a form that could be transferred to the computer.[5] Actually, this laborious process of accumulating information on and evaluating individual candidates dragged on to the very end of the search process in the following March. The blame for this lay mainly with us. We had never set a deadline for receiving applications or for responding to the advertisement in *Footnotes,* so that

4. A fourth half-time position came open to the department after our search to fill the three positions had been completed; it was ultimately filled with one of the candidates with whom we had established contact initially through the placement service. A description of the process leading up to this fourth appointment is given near the end of this chapter, under the heading "Postscript."

5. See Appendix C for a sample faculty evaluation form.

new inquiries and applications were coming into the office up to the time of our final deliberations. We continued to evaluate these late applications according to our standard procedures, on the dual assumptions that it would be fair to the candidates to do so (since we could not legitimately consider that they had failed to meet a deadline) and that it was still conceivable that very strong candidates would be found among the late applicants. The second reason for delays lay with the faculty evaluators. Reading files is not intrinsically a very rewarding activity, and the typical faculty member at any given time would prefer to be doing something else. Some evaluators were extremely prompt, but others tended to delay, for various reasons. For the Department office these months meant a campaign of prodding and sometimes harassing delinquent faculty members, sometimes at the cost of straining faculty-staff relations.

At this point in our story we pause to note three issues that occupied our attention in various ways during these months—finances, the computer, and the process of communicating with candidates and referees.

The Mode of Securing Financial Support for the Search: Begging

One of our earliest frustrations came in the area of financial assistance for the search. We anticipated the need for the rental of an automatic card typewriter and the computer. This request seemed modest in our estimation, amounting to no more than a request for a half-time clerical assistant, and totaling about $4,000 in all. To make such a request, however, we were required to make a justifying case to the campus administration. In this instance, this meant presenting a version of the "rational plan" outlined in the preceding chapter, with special underscoring of the advantages of the plan from an affirmative-action standpoint. Perhaps we made the case too well. The plan received an enthusiastic reception among the officials of the College's

Office of the Dean, but instead of offering funds that office recommended that we move to higher administrative levels and try to convince the affirmative-action office—located in the Office of the Chancellor—of its merits.

We met only limited success at higher levels as well. After some delay, we received word that the Chancellor's affirmative-action office would fund the computer portion of our request (about half the total) but would not provide funds for the typewriter. Instead, the affirmative-action office volunteered to let us use their own typewriter, which was, in any case, underused. Such an offer appeared impractical. The Chancellor's Office was located several blocks from our own, and the difficulties of carting the necessary papers to and fro promised to scuttle such an arrangement. We went again to the College of Letters and Science, pleaded our case once more, and argued that the affirmative-action office's proposal was unworkable. In the end the College officials agreed to pick up part of the cost of the typewriter, if we would squeeze the remainder from the Departmental budget.

Later in the search process we encountered another financial need for which we had no available resources in the Departmental budget: transporting and paying the expenses of candidates we wished to interview. The College would not guarantee such funds until we could demonstrate that we had a number of promising candidates we wished to bring. By late January we had such a list and approached the appropriate officials. But then a considerable delay occurred because the College split the request into two lists of candidates, one for minorities and women and another for "others," and forwarded the former to the Chancellor's Office with a request for affirmative-action support. In the meantime, the pressure of time dictated that we move ahead with the interviews. We did so, but the request for funds was not approved until after all the interviews had actually taken place.

In the end, it could be said that we were successful in generating financial support. The entire process, however, was time-consuming, fraught with uncertainty, and frustrating. Furthermore, the financial support was provided on a one-shot basis, leaving it to successors to go through the same process in later years. The one positive note is that the process produced a certain amount of interest in our procedures.

The Computer

The use of a computer as a method for rationalizing our filing, sorting, and evaluating operations proved to be both innovative and helpful. It enabled us to search through and sort our "files" on any one of the many pieces of information contained therein. We could, for example, at a moment's notice, determine which files were complete and which were not; what was required to complete the incomplete ones; how all candidates for one position had been ranked with respect to excellence of written work; how certain categories of applicants—blacks, for example—were faring in the competition. In fact, the computer produced much more than we needed; on one occasion, for example, it yielded a numerical average of the zip codes of all the applicants. On at least one occasion it saved Smelser from a minor humiliation. He had just completed a long-distance telephone call with a colleague in the East, who had phoned in his referee's comments on one of the candidates out of concern that a letter would not reach us in time. Smelser took a page or two of notes on the candidate, but neglected to jot down—and subsequently forgot—the candidate's name. We then asked the computer to produce a list of candidates from the referee's home institution, along with a list of their areas of specialization; comparing that list with the information Smelser had obtained from the referee, we were able to identify easily the name of the candidate in question.

Despite the evident usefulness of the computer, faculty reaction to it was mixed. Those faculty members whose work was in survey research and related fields were quick to appreciate the utility and efficiency of this particular aid. Indeed, they tended to press for the inclusion of much more information and finer distinctions than we believed necessary for the evaluation process. Other faculty members were skeptical. In most cases, this attitude was rooted in the vague apprehension that by using the computer, we the faculty were somehow losing control over the process, and that the computer was doing the selecting. Despite the erroneous basis of this apprehension—the computer was, in fact, only a very superior recorder and reporter of prior faculty evaluations—it lingered, and dissipated only with actual demonstrations of the computer's facilitating role as the committees proceeded with their work. At least one faculty member was preoccupied with the issue of confidentiality and secrecy, given the fact that we were using a time-share computer to which many other individuals had access. However, the computer was probably a more secure storage place than a file cabinet, for three reasons: first, we had a frequently altered code access known only to us; second, our identification number was accessible only through certain phone numbers; and, third, the various codes necessary to produce statements were unique to our data and known only to us. Despite these safeguards, this faculty member's anxieties persisted, and he continued to insist that an ingenious and motivated person might break through these levels of security to obtain information.

From the beginning, the "computerized" aspect of our search stirred a great deal of interest, both on the Berkeley campus and on other campuses. In light of this interest, we arranged a "dummy" file for demonstration purposes. Use of this file for these purposes assured the confidentiality of our own records. At the same time it was more convenient to use than actual records because it contained only thirty-five entries, and thus could complete the various sortings more quickly. We produced our first such demonstration for the Dean's Office and the affirmative-action office when we were attempting to persuade them to fund the operation. As word spread informally, we were asked to demonstrate the computer's utility to university management groups on the Berkeley campus, and to various friends and colleagues on the UCLA and Davis campuses. In January of 1976 we demonstrated the process to a university-wide meeting of nine sociology department chairpersons at UCLA. Most of these "road shows" evoked reactions of fascination and appreciation, though now and then a residue of skepticism would surface. About one month after the UCLA demonstration a candidate who had heard about it came to our office, announcing that she had been told that the Berkeley faculty positions were being filled by computer, and that she wanted to know what criteria were being used by the computer. This called for a short demonstration to dispel her suspicions, and to convince her that human judgment was, indeed, entering into the process.

Communicating with Candidates and Referees

Systematic evidence of "outside" reactions to our procedures was scanty. Still, we collected enough anecdotal evidence to offer some speculations.

The most important fact about the kind of search we were undertaking is that, despite our attempts to be as routine, straightforward, and fair as possible in gathering information, most of the candidates we communicated with were unaware of the actual procedures we were going through and, as a result, the whole process remained largely a mystery for them. Furthermore, many of the candidates were both highly motivated and very anxious about their chances in the competition. In such an atmosphere—combining uncertainty with high emotional loading—much is likely to be made of small cues. For example, we routinely requested letters of recommendation from all individuals listed on a candidate's curriculum vitae or submitted separately. From our point of view, this seemed essential if we were to give all candidates reasonably equal treatment. Yet on subsequent occasions we learned that some candidates who heard that their references were being contacted for letters occasionally interpreted this information as an indication that they had "passed" some critical level in the screening process. Similarly, when we routinely requested at least one sample of the candidate's written work, we later learned that this, too, was often interpreted as a further indication of having reached a "stronger" position. In response to such requests we would often receive letters or phone calls from candidates seeking advice as to what would be the "best" kind of written material to submit. Such reactions on the part of candidates suggest that their anxieties were very high, and that the air of great uncertainty in a buyer's market makes entry into that market a painful experience for many.

Early in the search certain problems of data-recording arose which required one additional form of communication from the candidates. We knew from the beginning that we were required by the University of California's affirmative-action procedures to provide information on the age, gender, ethnic identity, and fields of specialization of all the candidates. Yet we also discovered quite early that the material we were gathering routinely from all applicants did not yield accurate information with respect to these categories. While gender could very often be determined by first names, this was not clear in every case. Most applicants' résumés provided no information on ethnicity, and were often confusing or inconsistent with respect to their fields of specialization within sociology.

After agonizing over this matter, we decided that the only way to secure this information was to ask the candidates themselves, even though we realized that to do so might constitute an unwelcome intrusion and might arouse suspicion in their minds. We developed a brief questionnaire (Appendix D) and a covering letter explaining that compliance was strictly a voluntary matter. We also enclosed a list of standard fields of graduate study developed by the American Sociological Association, asking them to designate their fields of specialization by using those categories.

In the course of developing the questionnaire, it occurred to us that it might be judicious to clear its use with the central administration of the Berkeley campus. To our consternation, we were told that university policy forbade asking about sex and ethnicity. We faced a curious administrative doublebind, in which we were asked to submit reports containing data which we were prevented from securing. After an appeal, the administration gave us a special one-time-only permission to proceed with distributing the questionnaires.

Most candidates proved accepting of the questionnaires, with only 11 percent of those responding to the questtionnaire refusing to indicate gender and ethnic membership. We did uncover, however, certain evidence of resentment on the part of white males in responses, since this was the only category of respondents to give "silly" responses or to append irritated notes on the questionnaires.

We also learned a few things about what apparently happens to the refereeing process in a buyer's market. For one thing, the number of letters of reference multiplies. We ourselves initiated inquiries for more than a thousand such letters (many résumés contained the names of as many as eight or ten referees), sometimes asking a single colleague at another institution for as many as six or eight separate letters. We knew, moreover, that many of the candidates were making several applications—which also increase under buyer's market conditions—and that referees were having to write to those other places as well. (It is not uncommon these days for Berkeley graduate students attempting to find post-Ph.D. positions to write to as many as thirty or forty institutions.) We heard many grumbles from colleagues about the increased amount of time spent in placing students. We also received many obviously xeroxed, "To Whom It May Concern" letters. Occasionally we received a standard, fairly glowing letter of recommendation accompanied by a handwritten postscript indicating that the sponsor was actually reluctant to recommend that particular individual for a position at Berkeley. This suggested that such sponsors had not been completely candid with their students with respect to their expectations. On the other hand, we received occasional letters from candidates themselves indicating that Professor X had been "incorrectly" listed as a reference and should be deleted. This suggested, on the contrary, that some sponsors had indicated an unwillingness to write positively.

THE WORK OF THE SUBCOMMITTEES

We now pick up the story around the beginning of January, after each subcommittee had evaluated several dozen files and was in the process of reviewing more as they became complete. We asked the subcommittees to begin their meetings early in January and continue meeting as often as necessary throughout the month. Each subcommittee was given the straightforward though not necessarily simple task of identifying the three most promising candidates for their position. It was anticipated that these three would then be invited for interviews during the month of February. Because we were uncertain how many of these nine finalists (three for each position) would actually accept an invitation to be interviewed, we also asked that each subcommittee prepare a list of three or four alternates, who would be waiting in the wings, as it were, to be contacted for interviewing if the leading three candidates proved to be either unavailable or available but disappointing.

For their meetings, the committee members were provided with the files of all the candidates they had reviewed, including notes taken by the reviewers at the time of their readings. They were also provided with a computer printout supplying the names, institutional identification, and certain additional data on each candidate. The most important feature of this printout was that the computer had been instructed to rank-order the candidates in terms of excellence and promise, by pooling the evaluators' individual ratings on career pattern, letters of recommendation, and written work. The computer, in short, produced a summary statement of all the work that the evaluators had been doing individually over the past few months.

The printouts proved to be compact but enormously informative. The degree of consensus that had been arrived at independently and in advance could be revealed at a glance; discrepancies in evaluations could also be spotted quickly, and discussion could be directed immediately to the basis of disagreements among the evaluators; and it could be ascertained from the printout whether one particular feature of a candidate's file (written work, for example) was responsible for a high or a low ranking. Candidates who had been rated uniformly low could be identified easily, and this facilitated the shortening of the list in the early stages of the subcommittee's work. We might add that the computer's work proved to be a source of intense fascination to the evaluators, and much time was spent poring over the details of that work, even by those who had no particular love for computers.

In the later stages of each subcommittee's deliberations, interest focused on a group of ten or fifteen candidates from which the finalists and alternates would be chosen. The subcommittees did not simply follow the dictates of the computer in making those choices; rather, they discussed each candidate and moved his or her name up or down the ranked list on the basis of these discussions. By the second or third week in January each subcommittee had submitted a ranked list of some ten candidates each. The first three were regarded as the most promising, and were recommended for interviewing; the second three or four were first alternates; and an additional three or four were regarded as quite promising, but with some reservations. In addition, there emerged a category of candidates that we labeled "wild cards"—those who were extremely promising, but whose qualifications, training, and interests lay clearly outside the terrain specified by the "job descriptions" of the three positions, broad as those were. One such candidate showed exceptional strength in sociological theory, another in research on American national culture and institutions. These candidates, too, were kept in our minds as active candidates, to be invited if we faltered in our other efforts.

Given the general difficulty of gaining consensus on almost any issue in the Department—and personnel issues were among the most delicate—we were surprised to see how easily consensus was reached on the part of each subcommittee in nominating its leading candidates. The reasons for this are somewhat elusive, but the following considerations are probably relevant. Initially, the level of rater reliability attained in the independent review process was quite high, as inspection of the computer's results revealed. The reason for this, in turn, was that the members of each subcommittee were chosen to represent expertise in the respective areas of specialization (quantitative methods, comparative institutional analysis, urban sociology, and so on); correspondingly, the criteria by which each member assessed each candidate were probably quite similar. Yet, in addition, relatively easy consensus was attained in the subcommittee with the most diffuse charge—the demography and urban-stratification subcommittee—which cast its net very widely. Two additional reasons should be cited. First, we had gathered quite abundant—and comparable—information on each candidate, so the subcommittees were not plagued with the problem of having differing amounts of information on which to base their judgments. Finally—and by inadvertence—there was the circumstance that each sub-committee had been instructed to produce not only three leading candidates for interview but also some alternates. The alternates list probably eased the consensus-forming process, because placing a favored candidate on a list of alternates did not involve his or her complete rejection; the possibility of reactivation remained. We should add, finally, that these early moments of consensus in the small subcommittees were to prove momentary, and that the Departmental divisions once again became more salient as the decision-making process began to involve larger numbers of the faculty.

After the subcommittees completed their work, the personnel committee as a whole met to review their rankings and recommendations. It should be remembered that the chairperson of each subcommittee was also a member of the larger personnel committee, so that the rationale for the subcommittee's rankings could be readily summarized for the personnel committee as a whole. Sometimes, too, additional members of the relevant subcommittee were asked to participate in the personnel committee's deliberations. By and large, the personnel committee as a whole endorsed the recommendations of the respective subcommittees, and the stage was thereby set for the candidates' visits.

THE INTERVIEWS

For the visits themselves, we had a schedule that was to prove gruelling both for the candidates and for ourselves. We set aside every Tuesday and Thursday in the month of February to accommodate the nine potential visitors. Then Smelser called them and found that all nine agreed to visit. This perfect batting average no doubt reflected the drawing power of a major research-oriented institution like Berkeley, but perhaps more important, it constituted a commentary on the real and psychological tightness of the academic market in sociology. Graduate students believed that it was risky to turn down any reasonable opportunity that might present itself. We were somewhat surprised at the perfect acceptance rate because it was already late in the "season" of university interviewing and into the "season" of extending and accepting offers; many of our leading candidates had already been interviewed several times elsewhere, and some already had offers and semi-offers in hand when they arrived for our interview.

The typical visit went as follows: The candidate arrived, usually the day before the scheduled visit, having been sent an airline ticket and notified of appropriate room reservations in a nearby hotel. During the morning of the visiting day, the candidate met individually with faculty members whose interests and areas of expertise overlapped with his or her own. Usually all members of the relevant subcommittee and most members of the personnel committee would also meet individually with the candidate. In the middle of the day the candidate gave a formal presentation to a group of faculty members, graduate students, and a few undergraduates and people from other departments. The presentation typically included some facet of the candidate's doctoral dissertation research and was followed by a sometimes brisk exchange between the candidate and the group. Later at lunch perhaps seven or eight faculty members carried on further explorations with the candidate. The afternoon continued with individual interviews, and the last formally scheduled event was a meeting alone with graduate students, who carried on discussions and arguments with the candidate on sociological subjects. The day ended with a drink or dinner with a faculty member who had volunteered or been recruited to attend to the candidate. Sometimes the candidate would stay overnight, but more often he or she was deposited, in a somewhat numbed state, in a limousine bound for the airport.

We venture several impressions about these visits. First, they mattered. Even for those who had read and evaluated a candidate's material previously, new and strong impressions were generated during the individual interviews and the formal presentations. These impressions, furthermore, played a definite role in the subsequent rankings of finalists by the subcommittees, the personnel committee, the faculty as a whole, and the graduate students.

Second, for reasons not entirely clear to us, the visits more often than not generated more negative than positive reactions. Flaws in reasoning, inability to communicate, inadequacy in understanding and fielding questions, and offensive idiosyncracies of personal style—all presented themselves more vividly in first-hand encounters than they could possibly have done in the candidate's written dossier, which normally contains carefully prepared and sifted information. Perhaps, too, the psychological pressure created by public exposure to a potentially critical audience is likely to rattle an individual candidate and bring out the worst. This phenomenon might also be related to the fact that heretofore the individual had been evaluated mainly by those with overlapping areas of interest and expertise. By contrast, the gatherings of faculty members and graduate students were necessarily more heterogeneous, and a greater proportion of onlookers and interviewers would be likely to find fault with the particular design, style, or results of the candidate's research.

Third, we faced a problem of generating sufficient faculty participation in the visits. Most department members have many interests and obligations, and this leads them to shun some activities with which they should, in principle, concern themselves. In addition, some of the candidates were working in corners of research or using methods of research about which many faculty members knew or cared little. Finally, the number of visits itself was so great that it would have been too much to expect every faculty member to interview every candidate and to attend every presentation and luncheon. For all these reasons, Smelser had to assure that ample publicity was given to each visit, and to take the initiative in persuading individual faculty members to interview and to be present on various occasions.

Fourth—and this was a more personal, perhaps idiosyncratic reaction—Smelser found himself developing unusually friendly feelings toward every single visiting candidate, and wishing that we could appoint every one of them, unrealistic as he knew this was and aware as he was of the limitations of each. Introspection revealed that these feelings were based in turn on a positive identification with each of them. That identification was based, in its turn, on his sense of the brutalization that each visitor was undergoing. In one way, the visit was a reward; the candidate had been endorsed as one of the elect from a number of perhaps one hundred competitors. The psychological effect of that election, however, served not only to elate and give new hope, but also to excite new anxieties and fears of rejection. To ask a candidate to show his or her wares before an invariably critical audience who holds one's fate in its hands seemed one of the necessary but at the same time most painful features of the process.

The three finalists for each of the three areas of specialization were the following:

1. Under the demography and urban-stratification heading we considered first Candidate A, a female Ph.D. from an Eastern institution, whose dissertation had dealt with historical patterns of migration. Second was Candidate B, also from an Eastern institution; this candidate was categorized as "urban" largely because he had already completed a monograph on social life in an urban community. His dissertation dealt with conditions of factory life in a foreign country; for that reason, he might well have fit into the "comparative" position as well. Third was Candidate C, an advanced male graduate student at Berkeley, a macro-sociologist interested in the power of the Marxist notion of class in explaining and predicting various facets of individual behavior and attitudes.

2. Under the comparative heading we interviewed Can-

didate P, a male graduate student at an Eastern institution, whose dissertation involved an effort to explain the different patterns of accommodation and opposition in a wartime-occupied country. Candidate Q had earned a doctorate from an Eastern institution and currently held an appointment at one in the West; her dissertation had dealt with patterns of political activity on the part of various occupational groups in a revolutionary period. The third was Candidate R, a male graduate student at an Eastern institution, whose dissertation dealt with a social movement in a foreign country.

3. Under the quantitative methods heading, we considered first Candidate X, a male graduate student at a Midwestern institution, who commanded a wide range of quantitative techniques, and whose substantive work rested mainly in the analysis of social networks. We also interviewed Candidate Y, of the same institution, whose dissertation dealt with certain measurement problems involved in the analysis of social data. Finally, we gave consideration to Candidate Z, who held a Ph.D. from a Midwestern institution, but was currently on the faculty of a Western university; her interests were especially in the mathematical analysis of behavior.

The results of the interviews yielded such contrasting patterns of reactions that it is necessary to summarize each set separately:

The demography and urban-stratification position. The picture was clouded initially by the presence of Candidate C, our one candidate who was a Berkeley graduate student. From the very beginning of the search, the personnel committee had been of two minds. On the one hand, the Department had, in years past, sometimes recruited from the ranks of its own graduate students, and some strong appointments had been secured thereby. On the other hand, there was a discernible though somewhat diffuse sentiment among various faculty members that we should not hire our own graduate students. Early in its deliberations, the personnel committee achieved a kind of uneasy consensus on the matter: that we ought to make every effort to fill the positions from outside, but if one of our own students clearly emerged as the strongest candidate for any given position, that student surely should be ranked highest.

Candidate C received very positive evaluations from the demographic and urban-stratification subcommittee, and the personnel committee agreed that we should put him on the list of finalists for that position. We proceeded to schedule a regular "visit," in which he would make the usual presentation and talk with faculty members and students in individual and group situations, even though there seemed to be a certain awkwardness about such an arrangement, since most of us knew him well already. It never became clear, however, in the minds of those faculty members involved in the search exactly what role the prospect of "inbreeding" might ultimately play. Actually, the matter never presented itself to us directly; in early February, Candidate C received an extremely attractive offer from a leading Midwestern university, which he accepted. His "visit" was canceled, and inbreeding thus became one of the few issues we did not have to confront during the search process.

Only two candidates then remained for the demographic and urban-stratification position. But after their visits, it appeared that neither had generated great enthusiasm among a large number of faculty members. This left us with a problem: as of mid-February, it began to appear to the personnel committee that neither of the visitors in the demography and urban-stratification area would be likely to secure the support of a majority of the faculty. We experienced some alarm at this prospect, particularly given Smelser's earlier stress on the necessity to fill all the positions at the risk of their subsequent loss to the Department.

Accordingly, we broadened our sights for this position,

and activated two additional candidates. The first, Candidate D, was a graduate student at a Midwestern university. He had been considered originally by the "comparative" subcommittee, largely because of the research he had conducted on stratification in other societies. He had been ranked very highly by that subcommittee but had not found his way into the list of three finalists. At the suggestion of one of the members of the demography and urban-stratification subcommittee, he was brought to its attention, largely because of his interest in theories of stratification, as well as the topic of his dissertation, which involved a case study of industrial relations in an urban factory. The other candidate to be brought forward was Candidate E, a graduate student in history at a Midwestern institution who had come to the attention of one of the members of the personnel committee. Candidate E's dissertation was in the area of demographic and social history. By the time these two candidates emerged, however, it was late February. It would not have been possible for them to visit before March, and Smelser was growing increasingly apprehensive about the passage of time and the need to secure Departmental action and extend offers by early March, because of the danger of losing our preferred candidates to competing institutions. (Several of them were already holding other institutions at bay until they could hear from us.) Accordingly, no visits were arranged for Candidates D and E, but their names were put before the personnel committee along with those of Candidates A and B to develop recommendations for Departmental action.[6]

6. Candidate D had been on the Berkeley campus in early February, and a number of persons had attempted to persuade Smelser to arrange a presentation in place of Candidate C, who had already decided to accept the offer in the Midwestern university, and whose scheduled "visit" date had come open. Smelser declined to make this arrangement, because Candidate D was not on any final list at that time, and to schedule an interview would have been to extend special consideration to an "alternate." He and the chairman of the personnel committee did, however, interview Candidate D on an individual basis at that time.

The quantitative methods position. In this case another difficult situation confronted the personnel committee. Neither Candidate Y nor Candidate Z excited much faculty enthusiasm. Candidate X, on the other hand, drew a stronger but divided reaction. Most of the faculty members who themselves had quantitative skills and interests were very positively impressed, and voiced their conviction that he was by far the most able and qualified candidate in that area. Others who came to his presentation and interviewed him, however, believed that his work was narrow, both substantively and methodologically. Candidate X's formal presentation also drew a divided reaction. On the eve of the personnel committee's last meeting before preparing a Departmental recommendation, then, it was faced with the problem of having only one candidate it could reasonably present to the faculty as a whole, but knowing that his case might arouse controversy and possibly a divided vote.

The comparative methods position. The reactions to the visits of the three candidates for this position posed still another problem, though not as serious as the other two. Candidate R gave an interesting and informative presentation, but some faculty members regarded its scope as limited. Both other candidates, however, generated quite widespread positive responses. Candidate P revealed himself as a very gifted and imaginative interpreter of the situation of subordination during wartime occupation, as well as a general sociologist of breadth and cultivation. Candidate Q was regarded as having contributed a number of novel and important research findings relating to patterns of political participation in revolutionary activity. She, too, was perceived as an articulate and cultivated general sociologist. So positive was the reaction that a number of faculty members approached Smelser with the request that he propose to the campus administration that the Department recommend the appointment of *both* P and Q, with the promise that it would request one less position for the following year. Smelser resisted this request, partly on account of his conviction that the Department should honor the understandings it had originally made with the administration, and partly because of his reluctance to manipulate what he believed had been a relatively "clean" search process up to that time. Accordingly, he asked the personnel committee to come up with a single recommendation for the position in comparative sociology. The problem the committee then faced was: which of the two obviously excellent choices?

SECURING DEPARTMENTAL RECOMMENDATIONS

During the early reviewing and in the process of deciding which candidates should be brought for interview, the degree of consensus among the involved faculty members was, as indicated, quite high and was attained without protracted struggle and compromise. The visits, however, involved a broader band of interested constituents—more faculty members as well as graduate students—and, as a result, more heterogeneous judgments and more bases for disagreement and conflict became visible. Similarly, as the decision-making process now moved first to the personnel committee and then to the faculty as a whole, it became apparent that agreement was going to be more difficult to secure. In fact, in the days leading up to each department meeting and in the meetings themselves some faculty divisions crystallized, and academic politics came to play a more salient role than at any other time in the entire search.

As matters turned out, the timing of the three meetings was not a matter of our own choosing, but was forced upon us by external considerations. It became necessary to schedule the Departmental meeting on the quantitative methods position first, because Candidate X—the subcommittee's favorite—had in hand an offer from a leading national institution, which was aggressively pressing him to come to a decision by late February. The demography and urban-stratification position was considered second, because Candidate A and Candidate D both had outstanding offers; in particular, Candidate D was under pressure from a ranking national institution to indicate whether he would accept it by mid-March. There were no urgent pressures on the candidates for the comparative positions (each had other offers, but the offering institutions were not pressing for early decisions). In any event, the meeting on that position was scheduled to come last, since Candidate Q's visit was the last one, and no committee recommendation could be made to the Department until after her visit was completed. Because of these pressures, it became necessary to consider first those two positions that were most delicate and problematic.

Departmental tensions began to mount as the meetings approached, and all three meetings had the potential of creating a bitter division and ending in paralysis. Furthermore it was a likely possibility that if the first meeting—on quantitative methods—provoked such a division, it would carry over and possibly sabotage the subsequent meetings. In particular, Smelser was very apprehensive that the "humanist left" (see Chapter Five) would crystallize as strongly opposed to Candidate X, indeed possibly to *any* quantitative methodologist. Past votes and expressions of sentiment had convinced him that this was at least a possibility. Furthermore, he feared that if the quantitatively and scientifically inclined supporters of Candidate X were either defeated or presented with a large minority of opposing votes, they would likely close ranks and press, as a bloc or faction, for a quantitatively oriented candidate in one of the other positions. In particular, Smelser expected that a close vote in the meeting on Candidate X would promote a drive on behalf of Candidate A (the most quantitatively oriented of the demography and urban-stratification group), which would result in a closely divided vote for that position as well. A close vote in the meeting on Candidate X would also create the possibility that the quantitative methods group would unite in forceful opposition to Candidate D, who was quite evidently the humanist left's favorite for the demographic and urban-stratification position, in part because of his "Marxist" orientation. These possibilities were heightened when groups of graduate students produced two memoranda—one opposing the appointment of Candidate X, and a second favoring the appointment of Candidate D.

The situation with respect to the comparative sociology position did not cause Smelser as much concern, because neither Candidate P nor Candidate Q had generated strong opposition, and the Departmental expression probably would take the form of a preference poll rather than a politically polarized vote. There was a mild sense among some faculty members that Candidate Q was vaguely "left" of Candidate P, and this might become a basis of faculty division over their candidates. The shadow of affirmative action was also present: if the other two positions were filled, the likelihood would be that both of the appointees would be white males. In that event, and in the event that Candidate P were chosen for the comparative position, the Department would have ended with the appointment of three males and no minorities. The affirmative-action dimension was made explicit before the faculty meeting on the comparative position, when a committee of graduate students produced a recommendation that, on affirmative-action grounds, Candidate Q should be appointed, even though the students stressed the positive qualities of both Candidate P and Candidate Q. So, in the end, the possibility for a politically based faculty division emerged for the comparative position as well.

Smelser regarded the prospect of three divided meetings as extremely unwelcome. He was convinced, moreover, that the first meeting on the quantitative methodologist was by far the most crucial. In particular, he hoped that the recommendation for Candidate X's appointment could muster enough Departmental support to be a strong one. The situation in the personnel committee was as follows:

the committee itself was somewhat divided, with the majority supporting the enthusiastic recommendation of Candidate X by the subcommittee on quantitative methods. At least two members of that five-person committee, however, harbored some reservations; significantly, too, one of these was the member of the personnel committee who had closest ties with the "humanist left," the most likely group to crystallize against Candidate X. The divisions in the personnel committee, in short, constituted something of a microcosm of Departmental divisions, and appeared to preview the sort of debate that would develop in the faculty meeting. In the meantime, the graduate students' committee on methodology had taken a position in opposition to *all* the methodology candidates and recommended the appointment of none.

At this moment, Smelser made his only attempt of the entire search to intervene and influence the course of events directly. He attempted to persuade the chairman of the personnel committee—who up to this point was ambivalent about Candidate X—to speak publicly on behalf of him, mainly for "reasons of state." At the same time he contacted the most explicitly quantitatively and scientifically oriented member of the personnel committee, requesting him to attempt to assure the largest possible turnout of known supporters of Candidate X. Finally, he contacted the member of the personnel committee with the most solid links to the "humanist left" wing of the faculty, and attempted to convince him to persuade them to go along with the recommendation of the quantitative methods subcommittee, or at least not to oppose that recommendation. As the meeting approached, Smelser believed he had secured the cooperation of all those he had attempted to influence, but the outcome of that initial meeting was far from predictable.

At the meeting itself, the chairman of the quantitative methods subcommittee presented initially a strong favorable recommendation on behalf of Candidate X, followed by an eloquent and statesmanlike presentation by the chairman of the personnel committee, in which he acknowledged both unfamiliarity with and a certain lack of sympathy with the sociological style of Candidate X, but indicated that he was persuaded that those who were more familiar with that style had good reasons for a positive recommendation. As soon as the discussion was thrown open, however, the expected divisions began to make their appearance. Much of the discussion centered not around Candidate X's obvious technical qualifications—which were generally acknowledged to be very strong—but rather on his particular scope of interests and style of research. The discussion was civil but intense. The turning point of the meeting occurred when the member of the personnel committee with the best links to the "humanist left" announced that he would abstain from voting, largely because he was not familiar with Candidate X's style of research. At that moment the ultimate outcome appeared to be more nearly certain, and the final vote revealed a strong majority for Candidate X, along with a handful of abstentions.

The second meeting, for the demography and urbanstratification position, created a different order of problems. It will be recalled that Candidate C, the Berkeley graduate student, dropped out of the running after accepting a position in the Midwest, and that Candidates A and B had not generated much enthusiasm during the interview visits. The personnel committee had activated two additional candidates: Candidate D, the graduate student with a "Marxist" orientation in his work; and Candidate E, the historical and social demographer. At its meeting prior to the general Department meeting, the personnel committee reconsidered Candidates A, B, D, and E. There was still only limited enthusiasm for the first two, and, with respect to the other two, the personnel committee could not agree on which it should recommend; so it was decided to put both candidates before the faculty meeting, to indicate that the personnel committee was divided, and to have the candidates' respective merits discussed publicly.

Before the second meeting Smelser perceived solid support for Candidate D, not only from the "humanist left" but more generally. He also perceived some support for Candidate E as well, particularly among those who were committed to some variety of historical sociology as well as those who might have reason to find Candidate D's intellectual perspective uncongenial. He did not anticipate a confrontation at the second meeting, however, because both candidates were strong, and there did not appear to be a deep, principled opposition to either. At the meeting itself, however, an unanticipated turn of events occurred. Part way into the discussion, one of the quantitatively oriented faculty members reintroduced Candidate A (the demographer with quantitative skills) on grounds that she was technically more qualified, and showed more promise of making scholarly contributions to specific problem areas in sociology than did either of the other two. A few others joined in, supported her candidacy, and began to develop somewhat negative assessments of the work of Candidates D and E. Soon it became apparent that there was a measure of support for all three candidates, and that the poll of the faculty would be for three rather than two candidates. In the actual vote Candidate D received a bare majority, with the other two candidates splitting the remainder of the vote. There were no objections when Smelser interpreted the outcome of the meeting as indicating that he should approach Candidate D with an offer.

At that moment the situation became somewhat more relaxed. Smelser, along with several others, believed that either Candidate P or Candidate Q would receive a majority vote in the Department meeting on the comparative position, and that even if that majority were small, it would be appropriate to invite the winner to join the faculty, because support was so strong for both candidates.

The third meeting appeared to be a sort of "no-lose" situation, with the possible exception that if Candidate P were selected it would complete a phalanx of white male appointees. In any event, Smelser made no special effort to persuade any individual or group in the Department of the wisdom or desirability of supporting either one of those candidates. In fact, like many others, he was having difficulty making up his own mind.

At the meeting itself, the discussion was governed by the general sentiment that both candidates were of very high quality, and in the best of all worlds it would be desirable to appoint both. That possibility was again raised in the faculty meeting, but again resisted by Smelser. At that point, a general discussion of the two candidates ensued. As it turned out, even though most faculty members agreed on the excellence of both, each also had a preference. In the final vote Candidate Q received the very thinnest majority possible.

Each of the faculty meetings, then, produced a vote which could be read as authorizing the Chairman to proceed with offering a position to and negotiating with a single candidate. But in each case—with the exception of the third meeting—faculty members hovered on the brink of bitter confrontation and resulting paralysis. In retrospect, it appears significant that the Department was able to work with as many as three positions. As far as can be determined, there was no explicit "trading" of votes—"I'll vote for your favorite candidate if you'll vote for mine"—but the availability of several positions made it evident that most individuals and groups in the Department could expect to see the appointment of at least one candidate who was their favorite. Since that was the case, they were probably more likely to tolerate the recommendation of one or more candidates whom they did not regard as their favorites, or whom they might actively oppose if he or she were competing with other candidates for only one available position. The availability of several positions, in short, reduced the probability of a bitter struggle between factions.

Once the delicate process of Departmental politicking was concluded, the entire tone of the drama changed. The Department instantly changed its role from that of stern evaluator to that of ardent suitor. All three of the candidates whom we had selected had at least two alternative possibilities for appointment in other institutions. Some of these offers were more attractive in some particulars than our own. The problem now became one of convincing the candidate of our strengths and virtues, rather than vice versa.

As in the evaluation process, each case presented idiosyncracies. Candidate X, our choice for the quantitative methods position, had a number of offers outstanding, but the one that attracted him the most was from an Eastern institution which had great strengths in the very areas of his interest, and in which he had at least one close personal contact. In addition, that department was applying very strong pressure on him to make an early decision. About five days before the faculty met to consider the quantitative methods position, Candidate X telephoned us and explained that our competitor had given him a deadline for decision that was two or three days *before* our scheduled Department meeting—that is, before we would possibly be able to extend him a solid offer. Smelser urged him to convince them to extend the deadline, so that he would have the opportunity to consider all the options for his future career. He did obtain an extention of a few days, but not more. During those few days the other department continued to exert heavy and continuous pressure, and had actually secured an informal acceptance from him by threatening to withdraw the offer if he did not decide immediately. In the day or two before the Department meeting, Smelser made every effort to convince Candidate X that he had been unfairly influenced, and that what he had been persuaded informally to say could not be regarded as binding on him. Going out on a limb, he also told Candidate X that there was a high probability—he mentioned the figure of 90 percent—that the Berkeley faculty would vote to extend him an offer. This was admittedly a risky thing to say, because despite his and others' efforts to produce a consensus on Candidate X, Smelser had no real certainty that the Department meeting would not result in division and paralysis. Immediately after the Department meeting, Smelser telephoned Candidate X with the news of our offer, which he accepted immediately.

Candidate D presented less of a challenge, but a problem nonetheless. He was very much drawn to the Berkeley Department, and clearly preferred our offer to his others. He was somewhat mistrusting of us, however—and realistically so—because of what he had perceived as a cool reception in early February when Smelser was reluctant to take the occasion of his presence in Berkeley in early February to arrange a full-scale presentation and series of interviews.[7] After some assurance that he did indeed have strong support in the Department, he accepted forthwith.

Candidate Q was genuinely indecisive about accepting our offer. She had two other possibilities, neither of which were as desirable as Berkeley, but at which the competitive pressure would be much less. She feared a pressure-cooker situation in which she would be required to produce first-rate publications while trying to teach large undergraduate classes. She visited Berkeley after the offer had been extended, and talked at length with a number of faculty members. After being given assurance that she would have ample time to carry out her research projects, and after a period of indecision, she also accepted the position.

7. This situation has been commented on earlier, in footnote 6.

POSTSCRIPT A: A FOURTH POSITION

All during the search, Smelser had been engaged in informal negotiations with the administration and with the chairman of another social-science department regarding a joint appointment with sociology. The other department had for some time been under considerable pressure from the administration because of what was perceived as a poor showing with respect to affirmative-action appointments, particularly appointments of women. That department had located a woman candidate it wished to appoint, but was apprehensive that her appointment would absorb a position from another subfield in which the department was strongly committed to making a subsequent appointment. In the end, the administration and that department agreed that they would make the appointment if it could be done jointly, on a half-and-half basis with another department. By coincidence, their candidate had already applied to the Sociology Department for the comparative sociology position, and in that subcommittee's earlier evaluation had emerged near the top of the candidates. Once the administration approached us with the possibility of a joint appointment, then, the faculty approved her appointment after receiving assurances that it would not "count against us" in future negotiations, and that the candidate would not be disadvantaged in any way by having a joint appointment with another department.

AFTERTHOUGHT

The final results suggest that ours was a success story. We adhered reasonably well to the procedures we had set out in advance. We systematically reduced the field from approximately 285 applicants to 9 finalists, all of whom—except for our own graduate student, who accepted an offer elsewhere—agreed to come to Berkeley for a tour of mutual inspection. After this list of candidates—and two supplementary candidates—had marched in review, as it were, we further narrowed our list to a choice three, all of whom accepted our invitations. But as the unfolding story reveals, we maneuvered, staggered, and improvised throughout. There were many moments of near failure. The process cannot be well described as the unfolding of a plan, rationally conceived. Rather, it was a series of adaptive maneuvers executed within the context of a plan. The complicating features of real life continually intruded on the process. We daresay that this kind of picture is typical rather than unique. No plan, however carefully conceived, unfolds as a simple manifestation of the values and principles in the name of which it is devised.

What of the candidates who were not among the three? After the subcommittees had each presented to the personnel committee a list of some ten leading contenders, it became evident that the remainder were, for all intents and purposes, out of the running. What should be done about them? After a series of discussions it also became clear that the only appropriate course was to inform them, tactfully but unequivocally, that they were no longer candidates for consideration. We had no choice about what to tell them; it was only a matter of deciding when and how. In the end we decided to inform the unsuccessful candidates as soon as possible, in the interest of minimizing the element of agony that comes with waiting in an uncertain situation. Those below the "top ten" on each list were sent a letter indicating that they were no longer being considered, and that their materials would be returned to them. Those who were "alternates" or "wild cards" were sent another letter, indicating that they were no longer in the running, but that their names would be reactivated for next year's search if they so wished.

How does one reject 99 percent of those who have applied for a position? That task of rejection proved to be emotionally draining, as did the like assignment of rejecting dozens of candidates who telephoned to ask what their status was, whether we could arrange interviews, whether they should consider offers from other institutions, and the like. The letters of rejection—along with other facets of the search process—underscore one of its fundamental dimensions: it was a brutalizing process for many candidates, and many of its features can be understood as an effort to cope with that fact of brutalization. Furthermore, and ironically, one consequence of initiating an exhaustively thorough, fair, and public search—in which eighty or ninety times as many people will apply as will be taken—is that it increases the brutalizing aspect, because it subjects so many more to first hope, then uncertainty, then rejection.[8] The gains of an open and exhaustive search are many, and in the end that is probably the only form a search can legitimately take. At the same time, however, that kind of search also involves costs of anxiety and battered self-esteem among the many who suffer uncertainty and rejection, and costs of conscience on the part of those who subject them to those results.

8. For a bitter commentary on letters of rejection by a recipient, see Anna Ryan Nardell, "Deception in the Academic Job Market," *Change,* Vol. 9, No. 3 (March 1977), pp. 8–9.

CHAPTER 7

An Analysis of the
Pool of Candidates

Throughout our account of the changing conditions of the academic market, we have touched repeatedly on a number of themes. The first concerns the importance of prestige and influence in that market. Historically there has developed an extreme inequality of prestige among institutions; correspondingly, a relatively few institutions at the top of the hierarchy recruit primarily from one another but seldom from below. Does this condition still hold true? The second theme concerns self-selection. Do candidates receiving their training from less prestigeful institutions tend *not* to apply to more prestigeful ones, because they believe, realistically, that their chances for being hired by them are low?[1] The third theme concerns collegial networks. Are networks the main sources from which the stronger candidates are identified and recruited, and do weaker candidates make use of public sources, such as advertisements, because they lack sponsors who have network contacts? The fourth theme concerns affirmative action. Does reliance on traditional means of recruitment—largely by network—lead to effective discrimination against minorities and women because they are less visible members of that network?

1. For some anecdotal material on self-selection, see Chapter Six.

135

One by-product of our efforts to be as thorough as possible in seeking information on candidates and evaluating them is that we secured a wealth of facts that may throw light on those several themes. We now examine those facts in a variety of ways, prefacing that examination with the acknowledgment that ours represents only one case and should not occasion generalizations to the entire market for academic sociologists, much less the academic market in general.

INSTITUTIONAL ORIGINS OF CANDIDATES

From what institutions did our candidates originate? We attempted to answer this question from a variety of angles. First, we asked about the array of applicants according to the prestige of the institutions from which they received their doctorates. We identified the doctorate-granting institution for each applicant, and totaled the number of applicants for each institution. Then we listed these institutions in the order they were ranked in the national rating of "quality of graduate faculty" in the American Council on Education's survey published in 1970.[2] The results of these tabulations are found in Table 1. In all, almost three-fifths of our applicants came from those twenty-one institutions; that figure rises to nearly two-thirds if percentaged against the total number of applicants for which we had definite information on Ph.D.-granting institutions. Moreover, the "top six" account for more than half (54 percent) of those supplied by the twenty. Clearly there is a skewing of candidates toward the top, which creates a strong presumption that the "self-selection" principle was at work—those from less prestigeful institutions were not heavily represented to the response to a position publicized by a high-prestige institution.

2. K. D. Roos and C. J. Andersen, *A Rating of Graduate Programs* (Washington: American Council on Education, 1970), p. 69.

TABLE 1
Degree-Granting Institution of Applicants for
Sociology Positions at Berkeley and Michigan
(1975—76) by Ranking Institutions in
American Council on Education Survey (1970)

ACE Ranking	Institution	(285) [252][a] Berkeley Applicants	(275)[a] Michigan Applicants
1	Berkeley	8	17
2	Harvard	20	20
3	Chicago	21	16
4	Columbia	9	9
5	Michigan	17	4
6	Wisconsin	14	17
7	North Carolina	7	5
8	UCLA	8	2
9	Cornell	5	7
10	Johns Hopkins	6	3
11	Northwestern	6	6
12	Princeton	4	6
13	Washington-Seattle	3	3
14	Yale	6	6
15	Minnesota	5	10
16	Stanford	11	6
17	Michigan State	3	6
18	Texas	2	2
19	Indiana	4	9
20	Brandeis	4	2
21	Pennsylvania	2	5
	TOTAL	165	161
	Percentage of all Candidates	(58%) [65%]	(59%)

[a]Numbers and percentages in parentheses refer to total number of applicants; numbers and percentages in brackets refer to total numbers of candidates on whom information was available.

TABLE 2

Distribution of Berkeley Candidates and Average
Yearly Degree Recipients by Rank of Institution

Rank of "quality of graduate faculty"	Total doctorates, 1971–75	Average doctorates, 1971–75	Total percentage, 1971–75	Berkeley Candidates	Percent
Top six universities	536	107.0	16.4	89	35.3
Universities unranked from 7 through 21	804	106.0	24.6	76	30.5
Total, top 21	1,340	268.0	40.9	165	65.8
Total, remaining universities	1,933	386.6	59.1	87	34.3
Total, all universities	3,273	654.6	100.0	252[a]	100.0

Source: *Earned Degrees Conferred*, Institutional Data, National Center for
Educational Statistics, Washington, D.C., 1971–75 (Institutional
data unpublished for 1972, 1974, and 1975).

[a]Numbers and percentages based on Berkeley candidates on whom degree
information was available (252); total number was 285.

To provide further evidence on self-selection, we made
an effort to compare the distribution of total number of
Ph.D. degrees granted by different categories of graduate
institution with the distribution of such degrees among
our own pool of applicants. The results of this comparison
are shown in Table 2. On the average, the six top-ranked
institutions (listed in Table 1) accounted for an average of
about one-sixth of the total doctorates granted between
1971 and 1975; among our applicants, however, they
constituted one-third of the total. The twenty-one institutions listed in Table 1 produced about two-fifths of the
doctorates in those years; but they supplied nearly two-
thirds of our applicants. The remaining lower-ranked institutions were correspondingly underrepresented in our
pool.

One further set of data suggests that this pattern of
applications is quite general for institutions of Berkeley's

kind. We were able to secure comparable information from the personnel committee of the University of Michigan in their search for candidates to fill a number of assistant professor positions in the same year as our search, 1975–76. Michigan is a good "replication" institution, because like Berkeley it is a public institution that occupies a very high place in the "quality of graduate faculty" ratings. The Michigan data are also reproduced in Table 1. The two arrays are striking in their similarity. Not only are the total number and percentage of applicants from the "top twenty" almost identical; the numbers from each specific institution are very close to one another. The only exceptions to this similarity are found in an "anti-inbreeding bias," with few doctorates from Berkeley and Michigan applying to their respective home institutions, and a "regional bias," with Berkeley receiving more applications from UCLA and Stanford, and Michigan receiving more applications from Minnesota and Indiana.[3] We did not secure the names of the candidates in Michigan's pool; but the close resemblance of numbers originating from each doctorate-granting institution leads us to speculate that many of the same individuals appeared in both pools.

We also attempted to address the question of the institutional origin of our candidates by comparing our own faculty ranking of candidates by quality with the prestige of their doctorate-granting institution. Our ranking categories were "hired and/or interviewed" (n = 11), "strong but not interviewed" (n = 24), and "not strong" (n = 182). Next we sorted those candidates in four ranked categories of "prestige of doctorate-granting institution." Category I included six institutions in the highest range of rating scores on "effectiveness of doctoral program" in the 1970 ACE survey; Category II included fourteen institutions in the next range; Category III included twenty-two institutions in the next lower range; and Category IV in-

3. Such bias did not appear to extend to Northwestern and the University of Washington, however.

TABLE 3
Final Evaluation of Candidates and Research Quality of Ph.D.-Granting Institutions

Final Evaluation of Berkeley Candidates	Quality of Institution of Candidates									
	I		II		III		IV		Total	
	N	Percent	N	Percent	N	Percent	N	Percent	N	Percent
Hired and/or interviewed	8	11	3	5	0	—	0	—	11	5
Not interviewed but strong	10	14	8	13	5	20	1	2	24	11
Reviewed and not strong	54	75	53	83	20	80	55	98	182	84
Totals	72	100	64	101	25	100	56	100	217[a]	100

[a]Total is less than the grand total of candidates (285) because certain categories of "final evaluation" (for example, "withdrew or declines," or "incomplete file") were not included in the total.

cluded institutions that were "not rated" in the ACE survey.[4] The cross-tabulations of these rankings appear in Table 3, in which the skewing is even more marked than in Table 1. Three of the four appointees received their doctorates from the top category of institutions, and of the top eleven candidates—who probably constitute the total pool from which those finally appointed would have come—eight were from that category, and the remaining three from Category II. Almost every candidate from third-ranked (III) and unrated (IV) institutions fell into the "reviewed and not strong" row. Tables 1 and 3—especially the latter—generally confirm the principle that prestige institutions are likely to hire from other prestige institutions.

As a further exercise, we calculated the mean rankings that the candidates received from our faculty evaluators, according to the prestige of the institutions from which they came. The results of this exercise are arrayed in Table 4, and show the same type of skewing as Table 3. Looking at the bottom row, which includes the cumulative unweighted rankings on general career pattern, and samples of written work and letters of reference (see Appendix B), we find a steadily increasing mean score as we descend through the prestige ranks of institutions.[5]

We also analyzed the faculty evaluators' mean rankings based on each of the three ranking criteria separately. These are also included in Table 4.

Though all three categories are skewed in the same direction as the cumulative unweighted ranking—except for one small reversal between Categories II and III on "references"—an interesting difference between them appears. With respect to "career" rankings, the mean differences between types of institutions are greater than for the

4. Roos and Andersen, *Graduate Programs,* p. 69.

5. Since evaluators were asked to rank on a scale from 1 to 5, with 1 being the most favorable evaluation, a numerically low mean score signifies a favorable evaluation.

TABLE 4
Mean Faculty Evaluation Scores
for Candidates by Quality of Institution

| Types of Ranking | Quality of Institution | | | | |
	I	II	III	IV	Overall
Career	1.86	2.11	2.36	2.71	2.21
Written	2.28	2.36	2.37	2.74	2.43
References	2.13	2.16	2.10	2.49	2.23
Cumulative	2.09	2.21	2.29	2.65	2.29

other ranking categories, and the overall range of evaluations indicates a greater dispersal of the "career" rankings as well. This suggests that faculty evaluators, in assessing "general career"—which is usually done by studying the candidate's curriculum vitae—probably react to cues such as the individual's doctoral-granting institution, and a kind of "halo effect" develops as evaluators endow the candidate with a rank consistent with the level of prestige they attribute to his institution and its graduate faculty. This sort of effect is apparently not so strong in evaluating written work and letters of recommendation. We suspect that it would be even weaker if faculty evaluators read both written work and letters of reference "blind"—that is, without knowing the candidate's institution in the one case and without knowing the name and institution of his referee in the other.[6] In any event, the finding suggests the wisdom of not relying solely on the curriculum vitae for evaluation, since it apparently tends to produce somewhat more stereotyped judgments.

To round out our inquiry about institutional origins, we asked two final questions. (1) Is reliance on the network associated with the level of prestige of the Ph.D.-granting institution? (2) Is reliance on the network associated with our own final evaluation of the candidates? To throw light

6. The suggestion of reading written work "blind" came to us from Professor Robert Alford of the University of California, Santa Cruz, in a personal conversation.

TABLE 5
Source of Contact by Quality of Ph.D.-Granting Institution

			Quality of Ph.D.-Granting Institution							
	I		II		III		IV		Total	
Source	N	Percent	N	Percent	N	Percent	N	Percent	N	Percent
Network[a]	42	48	34	45	4	15	20	31	100	40
Public[b]	45	52	41	56	23	85	44	69	153	60
Total	87	100	75	101	27	100	64	100	253[c]	100

[a]"Network" includes contacts with department chairpersons, contacts with professional colleagues, applicants from Berkeley graduate students, and multiple sources which included any of the first three.

[b]"Public" includes responses to notice at the American Sociological Association meetings and responses to the public advertisement in *Footnotes*.

[c]Total is less than the grand total of candidates (285) because certain categories of contact (such as "unknown") are not included.

on the first question we divided our "sources" into two categories: "network," which included candidates produced from contacts with department chairpersons and professional colleagues, as well as candidates who were graduate students; the "public," which included candidates responding to the notice submitted to the placement service of the annual meetings of the American Sociological Association and to the advertisement in *Footnotes,* as well as a small miscellaneous category entitled "other," which was comprised of persons who submitted their names as candidates but did not identify the source from which they heard of the openings.[7] The level of institutional prestige was measured, as before, by the ACE rankings of "effectiveness of doctoral program" as published in 1970. The results of this cross-tabulation are found in Table 5. While the results of that array are not particularly striking, they are in the expected direction: as we move down the ranks of "institutional prestige" we find a tendency for those candidates located in the "network" search to decline in percentage, and a tendency for those candidates located in the "public" search to increase. This suggests—albeit weakly—that the network is, indeed, positively associated with the circulation of the names of candidates from prestigious institutions.

The suggestion contained in Table 5 is strengthened when we compare the source (network vs. public) with our final evaluation of candidates. Two-thirds of those candidates who were ultimately hired or interviewed were contacted through the network, whereas two-thirds of those labeled "reviewed and not strong" were contacted through public sources. The first datum is the more impressive, since three-fifths of all candidates whose sources were known came through public contacts. This skewing is represented in another way in Table 6, which shows that

7. As explained earlier, these categories of "network" and "private" are not entirely reliable, given the timing of our letter-writing and our public advertisements.

TABLE 6
Final Evaluation of
Candidates and Source of Contact

Final Evaluation	Network		Public		Total	
	N	Percent	N	Percent	N	Percent
Hired and/or interviewed	7	8	4	3	11	5
Not interviewed but strong	14	17	10	7	24	11
Reviewed and not strong	63	75	121	90	184	84
Total	84	100	135	100	219[a]	100

[a]Total is smaller than the grand total (285) because certain categories of final evaluation (such as "incomplete file") and certain categories of contact (such as "unknown") were omitted.

nine out of ten of those identified through "public" sources were not even considered as possibilities for interviews, and a majority of the strong candidates were "network contacts."

In sum, our data pertaining to institutional origin, quality of candidates, and mode of contact provided few surprises, and were largely consistent with the general themes noted at the beginning of the chapter. We discovered evidence of self-selection in favor of prestigious institutions, of higher-evaluated applicants coming from prestigious institutions, and of higher-evaluated applicants coming more from network sources than from public sources.

SEX AND ETHNIC CHARACTERISTICS
OF THE CANDIDATES

At the time of our search, the affirmative-action policies of the Berkeley campus called for a number of procedures to be followed in relation to the possible hiring of minorities and women. The first had to do with making the search as public as possible; concretely, this meant including one or more public advertisements that described the job, so that all could be given the opportunity to apply. The second had to do with modest kinds of encouragement and support for efforts to recruit minority and women candidates; the campus affirmative-action office, for example, provided funds enabling recruiting departments and schools to fly such candidates to Berkeley for interviews. Third, at the end of any search, a department or school was required to submit documentation describing the search, statements indicating why one candidate was preferred over others, and information regarding the sex and ethnic characteristics of candidates.

In our own search, we made every effort to conform scrupulously to these procedures, both because we believed them to be reasonable policies and because we were required to do so. Beyond that, we did not pursue an especially aggressive search for women and minorities, though all those who applied were given as full and equitable an evaluation as possible. We did not make a special effort to expand the pool of minority and women candidates beyond publicizing the position fully and including some special affirmative-action language in the advertisements and letters of recommendation (see Appendix A). During the evaluation phase of the search, sex and ethnic considerations apparently carried little weight in faculty evaluators' minds. Information on sex and ethnic identity was not supplied to individual faculty evaluators (in many cases it had not yet been supplied by the candidates), though in some cases it could be determined by knowing the name of the candidate or by noting some other identifying fact in the curriculum vitae. In the deliberations of the subcommittees, note was sometimes made of the sex or ethnic membership of the candidates, but to our knowledge no effort was made to "move" any candidate or class of candidates up or down the ranked lists because of their sex or ethnic characteristics. Committee and Departmental discussions focused mainly on the candidates' academic qualifications and promise, and only in the discussions of the relative merits of Candidate P and Candidate Q for the comparative sociology position was the argument raised in favor of hiring Candidate Q, a woman, on affirmative-action grounds.

In assessing the fate of minority and women candidates in our search, we asked several kinds of questions. How many minority and women candidates ultimately entered the pool of candidates? Did public sources yield a higher proportion of these candidates than network sources? From what kinds of Ph.D.-granting institutions did they originate? Did minorities and women receive consistently higher or lower ratings in the faculty evaluation process?

As indicated earlier, we believed it essential to request the sex and ethnic identification of the candidates who applied for our positions, and after securing permission from the administration, we did ask them to voluntarily supply that information. From the 285 candidates, we received responses from all but 74 candidates. Those 74 included both non-respondents and candidates whose applications had arrived too late for processing. The operative figure that constituted the basis for our subsequent analysis was, then, 211. Of that number, 32 simply refused to give ethnic identification. Of those who identified themselves, 154 were "Caucasian" or "White," and 25 were ethnic minorities (six blacks, four Hispanic Americans, 11 Asians, one Native American, and three "other").

We might speculate that few minorities and women were represented among those who did not respond at all, as well as among those who refused to give ethnic or sex information. For one thing, in the atmosphere of affirmative action, it was generally regarded to be marginally advantageous to be a minority member or a woman; insofar as this expectation existed, it constituted a stronger motive for minorities and women to identify themselves and for others to conceal their identity. More direct evidence in favor of this speculation is found in the evidence of some hostility, reported earlier, in white males' responses to the request for sex and ethnic information.

Whatever the composition of the non-respondents and those who refused to give information, we were struck by the small absolute number of minority applicants represented among candidates, particularly given our efforts to cast the recruitment net widely. We could not know, however, whether our reaction was an appropriate one, because we do not possess adequate data on the total available pool of minority sociologists in the nation who might be "in the market" for a position of assistant professor at Berkeley. We speculate, however, that the low turnout—if it was indeed low—rested both on the limited number of available minority candidates among new and recent Ph.D.'s and on the probability that many minority candidates "self-selected" themselves out of the running.

We can be more definite, however, on another kind of skewing according to minority status, which has to do with the source through which they initially came to our attention. Of the 74 candidates yielded by writing professional colleagues around the country—the strongest measure of the "network"—none was identified as black and only one was identified as Hispanic American. Furthermore, among the total of 105 candidates gained by writing to professional colleagues and chairpersons combined, only one black and one Hispanic American appeared. The remaining eight persons in these minority categories were identified through public channels of advertising. While this result is based on a very small number of cases, it suggests that minorities are less likely to be identified through network contacts, even if every effort is made to contact a large number of persons in the network, and even though attention is called to an interest in considering minority and women candidates.

To follow this hunch, we calculated the percentages of different categories of candidates that appeared from network sources and from public sources. Two sets of calculations proved consistent. First, of the twenty-five minority applicants, 28 percent were identified through network channels and 72 percent through public channels; of the candidates identifying themselves as "Caucasian" or "White," 41 percent appeared through the network contacts and 59 percent through public contacts. Second, of the total network contacts, only 9 percent were minority and 79 percent white (12 percent refusals); of the total number of public contacts 14 percent were minority and 69 percent were white (17 percent refusals). While these figures are not earthshaking, they do suggest that the network is less likely to produce minority candidates than public efforts to recruit. And if this observation is made with respect to two of the most disadvantaged minorities traditionally—blacks and Hispanic Americans—it indicates that the network is not a productive source, unless perhaps those categories are explicitly called for in requesting names of candidates.

With respect to sex identification, a different picture appears. Of our 285 total candidates, 212 responded to the request for information on sex; of these 20 declined to give that information. The total number on which we had definite information was 192; of that total, 49, or 26 percent, were women. (The actual percentage is slightly lower, since inspection of the names of those who declined to state their sex indicated that the preponderance were males). As with minority candidates, it is difficult to know whether this figure is low or high, because we had no direct access to the total pool of women candidates who might be available for appointment as assistant professor at Berkeley.

We were also interested in whether the network sources tended to produce lower proportions of women candidates than public sources, as they did in the case of minorities. This proved not to be the case. Of the forty-nine women on which we had definite information, 43 percent were identified through the network and 57 percent through public contacts; of the men, 37 percent were identified through the network and 63 percent through public channels. Moreover, when we considered the proportions of men and women candidates produced by network and public channels, respectively, the percentages were almost identical, as Table 7 shows. If anything, network sources tended to be very slightly skewed toward producing women candidates, indicating that they do not appear to have the lack of visibility that is apparently experienced by minority candidates.

TABLE 7

Sex Identification by Source of Contact

	Network		Source Public		Total	
Sex	N	Percent	N	Percent	N	Percent
Female	21	27	28	21	49	23
Male	53	68	90	67	143	67
Declined to state	4	5	16	12	20	9
Total	78	100	134	100	212[a]	100

[a]Total is amller than the grand total (285) because of a number of non-responses.

In a related line of questioning, we asked whether there was any systematic tendency for institutions of higher prestige to provide a lower proportion of minority and women candidates to our total pool. To answer this, we cross-tabulated institutions assigned to different ranks in the American Council on Education ratings with sex and ethnic status. The results are shown in Tables 8 and 9. With the possible exception of the slightly higher proportion of minorities whose Ph.D.'s were granted in Category III institutions, there is almost no skewing: the percentages of minorities and women who received their Ph.D.'s from each ranking category is almost identical to the proportion of minorities and women in the total sample.

Finally, how did minority and women candidates fare in the faculty evaluation process? To determine this we classified our candidates according to type of final evaluation—"hired and/or interviewed," "strong but not interviewed," and "not strong." We then cross-tabulated

TABLE 8

Ethnicity by Quality of Ph.D.-Granting Institution

Ethnicity	Quality of Institution									
	I		II		III		IV		Total	
	N	Percent	N	Percent	N	Percent	N	Percent	N	Percent
Minority	7	10	7	11	5	21	6	12	25	12
White	51	73	50	78	14	58	38	76	153	73
Declined to state	12	17	7	11	5	21	7	14	31	15
Total	70	100	64	100	24	100	51	101	209[a]	100

[a]Total is less than the grand total of candidates (285) because of non-responses.

TABLE 9
Sex and Quality of Ph.D.-Granting Institution

| Sex | Quality of Institution | | | | | | | | Total | |
| --- | I | | II | | III | | IV | | | |
	N	Percent	N	Percent	N	Percent	N	Percent	N	Percent
Female	17	24	16	25	4	17	11	22	48	23
Male	47	67	44	69	16	67	35	69	142	68
Declined to state	6	9	4	6	4	17	5	10	19	9
Totals	70	100	64	100	24	101	51	101	209[a]	100

[a]Total is less than grand total of candidates (285) because of non-responses.

TABLE 10
Ethnicity and Final Evaluation

	Ethnicity							
	Minority		White		Declined		Total	
Final Evaluation	N	Percent	N	Percent	N	Percent	N	Percent
Hired and/or interviewed	2	8	5	3	4	13	11	5
Not interviewed but strong	2	8	12	8	7	23	21	10
Reviewed and not strong	21	84	128	88	20	65	169	84
Total	25	100	145	99	31	101	201[a]	99

[a]Total is less than grand total of candidates (285) because candidates of unknown ethnicity were not included and because not all categories of final evaluations were included.

these categories according to the sex and ethnic identity of the candidates. Table 10 shows the percentage of minority and "white" candidates in each of the three categories. The percentages are very close to one another, indicating that ethnic minorities fared approximately the same as others in the evaluation. We note that those thirty-one candidates who "declined to state" their ethnic membership tended to score somewhat higher on the faculty evaluations than those who so identified themselves. Such a result provokes interest, but it is difficult to interpret because of the unknown ethnic identity of those who declined. However, even if we assume that all those who declined to state were "whites" fearing reverse discrimination on affirmative-action grounds, the numbers are sufficiently small that the overall percentage distributions would not be greatly altered. A similar picture is revealed for sex distribution in Table 11. The percentage of men and women in each evaluative category is very close, with women faring slightly better. Again, those nineteen who declined to state sex identity were slightly more favorably evaluated than those who did, but in this case the numbers are even smaller and the effect on the overall distribution even more

TABLE 11
Sex and Final Evaluation

					Sex			
	Female		*Male*		*Declined*		*Total*	
Final Action	N	*Percent*	N	*Percent*	N	*Percent*	N	*Percent*
Hired and/or interviewed	4	9	6	4	1	5	11	5
Not interviewed but strong	5	11	11	8	5	26	21	10
Reviewed and not strong	38	81	118	87	13	68	169	84
Total	47	101	135	99	19	99	201[a]	99

[a]Total is less than the grand total of candidates (285) because candidates of unknown sex were not included, and not all categories of final evaluation were included.

insignificant. In sum, these two tables reveal no obvious systematic skewing upward or downward of evaluations according to sex or ethnic characteristics.

CONCLUSION

In summarizing, we might return to the several themes mentioned at the beginning of the chapter, and ask what apparent effect our much publicized recruitment effort had on the search. Or to put the question in another way, how did the outcome differ from what it would have been if we had not introduced the public component?

The public search certainly augmented the numbers of candidates who applied, increasing them by approximately one and one-half times more than the number yielded by network contacts. Yet largely through the process of self-selection, we believe, the resultant total number was skewed toward applications from high-prestige institutions. Furthermore, and more decisively, that skewing intensified during the evaluation stage, with the vast majority of those candidates considered as strong, then interviewed, and finally hired concentrated progressively in high-prestige institutions. Of the three appointments finally made for the three allotted positions, two had received their Ph.D.'s from Chicago and one from Harvard—both Category I institutions in the ACE ratings (the fourth, a joint appointment with the other social science department, received her Ph.D. in Political Science from Stanford University). Other measures of faculty evaluation yielded similar results.

In comparing those candidates located through the network with those located publicly, the former tended to be skewed toward high-prestige institutions, thus indicating that the network operates more intensively among those institutions. And when evaluated, those located through the public advertisements fared less well than network candidates. As for affirmative action, the public advertisements turned up a much greater proportion of minority candidates than the network did, but the same was not true for women candidates. In both cases the absolute number of candidates was not high, but the reasons for this are obscure. Once activated as candidates, neither minority group members nor women appeared to fare either better or worse statistically than the generality of candidates.

CHAPTER 8

Some Reflections in Conclusion

In this chapter we review the institutional context of the search we conducted, reinterpret some facets of our search in relation to that context, and develop a few evaluations and recommendations that appear to flow from our analysis and experience.

RECENT CONTOURS OF CHANGE
AFFECTING ACADEMIC RECRUITMENT

One convenient starting point for tracing the most crucial economic, political, and social changes that have affected the academic market is to return to the analysis of Caplow and McGee, whose influential book constituted a backdrop for our earlier discussion of the market for Ph.D.'s (in Chapter One). Their argument, it will be recalled, was that the main basis for recruitment was *personal influence;* that is to say, people were hired because someone knew them, or because someone knew someone who believed them to be promising, or because someone important sponsored them. The dynamics of the marketplace, accordingly, are the dynamics of *collegiality.* A corollary feature of the collegial model is that the market is characterized by a low level of information, both about positions available and about candidates to fill them. Most communication is informal, as reliance is primarily on the opinions of important people about the future promise of some candidate. Given this dominant pattern, it is not necessary to publicize positions and to accumulate information about the largest possible range of candidates. A second corollary feature of the collegial model depicted by Caplow and McGee is its procedural informality and its lack of bureaucratic elaboration. As with the case of information, the dynamics of collegial influence provide a simplified functional substitute for bureaucratic processing, and render it unnecessary, except as a kind of afterthought for decisions already made. In addition, Caplow and McGee regarded the model of collegial influence as operating in relatively pure form, uncontaminated by other considerations. The conception of a special place for previously disadvantaged categories of candidates, for instance, found no place in their analysis; by and large their notion of academic search was a search simply for promising men. Finally, we should note that the setting for Caplow and McGee's treatment was one of extremely rapid expansion of academic positions, and, correspondingly, a seller's market for academic services.

Keeping in mind our judgment that Caplow and McGee's analysis was probably overdrawn even at the time it was written, we might nevertheless profitably ask: What are the major ways in which processes of academic recruitment have come to *deviate* from that model of collegial influence in the two decades since it was propounded?

A second starting point for addressing the same question is a recent analysis of the main lines of higher education by Talcott Parsons and Gerald Platt.[1] While their work ranges over a multitude of topics, we are particularly interested in their arguments concerning the functional primacy of institutionalized values in the university system. Focusing on "the arts and sciences subsystem" (which

1. Talcott Parsons and Gerald M. Platt, *The American University* (Cambridge: Harvard University Press, 1973).

includes graduate training and research as well as undergraduate teaching), they characterize the dominant organizational form of that subsystem as a "fiduciary collegial
association." The term "fiduciary" refers to the fact that
the primary focus of faculty responsibility is "to cognitive
standards and their implementation through processes of
critical evaluation," particularly in relation to professional
standards but also in relation to graduate and undergraduate teaching.[2] The term, "collegial association" refers
primarily to a type of social organization in which "membership is not attained either by universalistic ascription
[as in the case of citizenship in a polity] or entirely by
personal choice [as in the case of membership in a voluntary association] but by admission or appointment."[3] Colleagues in association are equal as peers, but the academic
system is regarded by Parsons and Platt as stratified into
layers (non-academics, undergraduate students, graduate
students, junior faculty, senior faculty, and so on) according to the degree to which they have been socialized into
and partake of the competence in and fiduciary responsibilities for academic standards.

While Parsons and Platt's language differs from that we
employed earlier, their emphasis is consistent with our
stress on the centrality of excellence in science and scholarship as the dominant institutionalized value of the
graduate and research-training complex, and is also consistent with the associated stress on prestige as the main
reward in that complex. Furthermore, Parsons and Platt
note that this dominant emphasis "skews" the recruitment
process away from a primarily economic market:

Though most colleges and universities operate employment services, services of graduates are not usually marketed by the
institution but constitute individual choices and arrangements.
Institutional involvement is stronger at the graduate-school than
at the college level, but even at the graduate-school level mainly

2. Ibid., p. 127.   3. Ibid., p. 143.

through evaluative recommendations by faculty members. Academic employment has in common with other cases where the employment agency is a collectivity that employment carries with it a status of membership in the employing organization, though at faculty levels this membership status is different from the ordinary status of worker.[4]

Thus, while Parsons and Platt's analysis differs in many regards from that of Caplow and McGee—and certainly they differ in their evaluative posture—both sets of analyses identify collegiality and its associated dynamics as lying at the heart of the academy of higher education.

As important as Parsons and Platt's positive characterization of the university is their corresponding rejection of several competing models as "not highly relevant" to its organization. These models are:

[an] economic market—the faculty are producers, the students consumers . . .

[a] bureaucratic organization—the trustees and top administrators are bosses, faculty members are middle-level and lower executives, students are the workers who have to obey orders . .

[a] democratic association where all involved are in principle equal participants or citizens, including sometimes not only faculty and students, but employees without any academic qualifications or goals.[5]

While acknowledging that these models are "admittedly caricatures," they criticize each on the grounds that it is not consistent with the dominant values of fiduciary responsibility for values of cognitive rationality. The major "consumers" of disciplinary knowledge, they argue, are not students; the major arena in which the acceptability or unacceptability of academic knowledge is determined is among professional colleagues on a national or international basis. The model of formal bureaucracy, which is

4. Ibid., p. 126.   5. Ibid., p. 125.

characterized as relying on authority and power as coordinating mechanisms, is also inconsistent with the dominant emphasis on specialized knowledge in institutions of higher education:

The realistic capacity of the bureaucratic executive to understand the problems involved at every level and in every part of the organization is a condition of the effective centralization of authority. But a university president or dean cannot understand more than a small part of the substantive intellectual problems confronted by the members of his faculty. Bureaucratization would necessitate confining the scope of a faculty to a small sector of the universe of knowledge, whereas the actual organizational tendency has been the reverse: the broadening of faculty responsibility as the range of knowledge has broadened.[6]

Correspondingly, faculties must be allowed a degree of autonomy in dealing with their respective subject matters, including autonomy in making decisions about whom to recruit as colleagues. And finally, the incorporation of all relevant constituencies as political participants is inconsistent with the stratification inherent in the fiduciary collegial association. "The obstacle to implementing [the pattern of democratic association] lies in the role of special knowledge and competence which comes from training and experience; a flat equalization of participatory rights means that newly entered freshmen and senior professors may not occupy different status in the governance of the institution."[7]

The arguments of Parsons and Platt are compelling on the general grounds that any attempt to maximize or even realize the features of the three competing models would threaten or even negate the core institutionalized values of the graduate training and research complex in universities. That being acknowledged, however, it must be reaffirmed that universities *do* have economic, administrative, and political features in their organization, and, more impor-

6. Ibid., p. 128.   7. Ibid., p. 129.

tant, that these features are not fixed but variable in their significance.[8] Furthermore, as they vary, they change the definition of the academic situation, and constitute exigencies that influence the execution of academic activities, including the recruitment of new personnel. We shall now argue, in fact, that in the past two decades all three of these kinds of exigencies have *increased* in salience, and have superimposed themselves more forcefully upon the collegial principle, thereby diminishing the degree to which that principle can be relied upon as an uncontaminated basis for academic recruitment. As we advance these arguments, moreover, we shall be simultaneously addressing the question of how contemporary conditions have deviated from the collegial model advanced by Caplow and McGee.

The Economic Dimension: The Implications of Diminished Growth for the Academy

The academy of higher education in the United States is now in a period of reduced growth or stagnation, following a period of exceptionally vigorous growth. The period of growth was characterized by general financial and political support, by a season of rising expectations, by innovation, and by the generation of new units in the system—new roles, more incumbents to fill these roles, new organizations, and new systems of organizations. (In the academic example this would be new faculty positions, more individuals filling them, new campuses, and new systems of campuses.) These new components constitute the structural base necessary for increasing the performance of the system (that is, educating more students, producing more research, providing greater service to the community and society, and so on).

Paradoxically, when the demands for growth on the part of any system slacken, *the structural base of that system does not automatically decrease at the same rate as the*

8. Neil J. Smelser, in ibid., p. 102.

decrease in demand for performance. Vested interests have crystallized among holders of the new positions, and those vested interests constitute a source of political and economic claim on the larger supporting system. The social-structural base that is created in a period of institution-building thus becomes a source of rigidity and inflexibility when that phase gives way to a period of reduced growth. That base, once necessary for a growing system to perform up to expected capacity, now becomes analogous to excess capacity.

The principle just enunciated applies in an exaggerated way to the present system of higher education in the United States. The reasons for this are rooted in the following considerations:

1. Many constituencies in the academy are not inclined to give highest priority to market or economic considerations. As we noted earlier, the value of excellence in science and scholarship is paramount in research and graduate-training centers, and these centers strive continuously to increase their relative prestige by maximizing that excellence. The continued striving toward excellence, moreover, impels the system toward increased development and increased support, which runs counter to the budgetary requirements of a diminished rate of demand for the system's services (specifically, for the teaching of students).

2. The academy, by virtue of its institutional position, does not have ready mechanisms by which it can reduce its structural base quickly. Particularly in the public sector, universities and colleges are not simply allowed to go bankrupt, as would a small business, when demand diminishes or when the quality of its performance falls below par. To drive a campus or university out of business requires a *political* as well as an economic decision, and those responsible—most often, state legislatures and state executives—are subject to political pressures not to make such decisions, not only from the universities and colleges themselves, but also on the part of the communities and regions in which they are located.

3. Higher education has institutionalized a number of structural arrangements—for example, the protection of academic freedom—which, in addition to their intrinsic academic significance, constitute rigidities to the downward adjustment of the structural base of higher education. We mentioned tenure especially, which effectively blunts the strategy of "laying employees off" as a way of dealing with reduced demand. (This factor is particularly significant at the present period of the academy's history, with such a high proportion of faculty "tenured in" as a result of the increase in appointments during the period of rapid growth.) We also mentioned a number of other structural elements that discourage turnover—annually based contracts, constrictions on "raiding" faculty from another institution, welfare benefits that discourage moving, and the like.

4. Many parts of higher education—particularly arts and sciences departments, including sociology—are "self-supplying," in that the teachers of the subject are employed in the same category of institutions (colleges and universities) which produce them. Graduate-training programs are thus analogous to an "investment industry" for the industry of college teaching. This circumstance—plus the long period for training a Ph.D. and a subsequent lag effect of six to ten years after a decision to produce or not produce has been made—means that in periods of diminished demand the academy will be faced not only with a potential for excess capacity but with a tendency to *continue to increase* that capacity despite reductions in demand, thus further aggravating the dislocation between supply and demand.

5. Colleges and universities are under pressure to increase certain *kinds* of recruitment, particularly from categories of minorities and women which have heretofore been little represented in the ranks of the faculty. Although such pressures do not necessarily entail an absolute increase in numbers of appointments, they do run counter to a policy of no-growth, since the goals of affirmative

action can be realized only with great difficulty if little recruitment is being done.

Such are some of the constraints that have contributed to the diminishing demand for Ph.D.'s, their continuing great supply, and the inability of the market to bring supply and demand into equilibrium. Translated into visible, everyday constraints for the administrator and faculty member, these market phenomena mean that vastly increased numbers of candidates make themselves available for a decreased number of positions, and that successful placement for new Ph.D.'s by faculty members and placement services is becoming increasingly more difficult.

The Political Dimension: The Increased Salience of New Constituencies for the Academic Department

From time to time in our analysis we have noted the existence of politically significant constituencies whose presence must be taken into account in one way or another in departmental recruiting. We mentioned, for example, the presence of the affirmative-action office on the Berkeley campus, which constituted a visible symbol of the pressures on the campus to take those kinds of goals into account in academic recruitment; we mentioned the presence of more or less organized groups of graduate students, whose voice was also heard from time to time as our recruitment proceeded; and we mentioned the complex pattern of faculty cleavages and factions that posed such a challenge to gaining consensus in the recruitment process. The presence of each posed a complicating feature in our political situation.

Regarding the political dimension more generally, we argue that in the past two decades the political forces affecting the conduct of academic life have become more significant and more complex, as old constituencies have increased in political salience and new ones have come on the scene. The major sources of this altered political situation are the following.

First, the years of social and political ferment of the 1960s and early 1970s precipitated—as deep, prolonged conflicts typically do—a number of new groups that continue to have a political significance even after the period of turbulence has receded. Restricting our view to the Berkeley campus, the late 1960s saw the crystallization of a higher level of political consciousness on the part of both graduate students and undergraduates, the emergence of numerous ethnic-based caucuses (black, Chicano, Asian American, primarily), and the emergence of a number of women's groups at different levels of campus organization. The demands of many of these groups were given added influence by friendly voices in political bodies such as the California state legislature, and by political pressure from "official" affirmative-action sources such as the Department of Health, Education, and Welfare, and community groups in the San Francisco Bay Area that took a political interest in the University of California's policies. Some of these groups have receded in salience as the years of conflict have given way to a less turbulent period. Nevertheless, organized groups such as the student lobby in Sacramento, groups of graduate students on the Berkeley campus, and various affirmative-action groups still remain, and enjoy a political status that is more significant than in the years before the political crisis that generated them.

Second, the emergence of such new political groups invariably generates a certain amount of "counter-movement" activity on the part of those who regard the goals of the new groups as antipathetic to the values of the university as they see them. This counter-movement activity takes a variety of forms, but the most salient for the academic department is the crystallization of groups of "academically conservative" faculty members who insist on the maintenance of traditional academic standards, and on the preservation of traditional collegial autonomy in determining faculty policy and executing faculty action. The new political groups, in short, constitute a challenge to the kind of stratification system described by Parsons and Platt. Those faculty members who welcome that challenge and those who oppose it gravitate toward different political camps, and these camps complicate the political life of academic administrations with respect to a wide range of academic policies and decisions, including academic recruitment and promotion.

Third, the enforcement of budgetary stringency in the period of diminished resources during the past decade has provided yet another set of political forces in the academic environment. In a direct sense, the flexibility of academic departments has been diminished by political decisions restricting the numbers of new appointments they can make, and restricting those appointments mainly to junior levels. More indirectly, political decisions limiting cost-of-living increases in faculty salaries affect administrators' ability to recruit by altering the conditions of work, as do threats to increase the faculty workload by mandating increased numbers of "contact hours" between faculty members and students.

Finally, we mention new kinds of faculty organizations as complicating elements in the political life of a university. We make little of this point, since faculty unionization has tended to make little headway in the large graduate-training and research centers such as the Berkeley campus. Most of its advances have been at primarily undergraduate teaching institutions. We should mention, however, the presence of a small but active chapter of the American Federation of Teachers on the Berkeley campus, as well as the Berkeley Faculty Association, an organization of between 400 and 500 members, which formed early in the 1970s in direct response to a series of state actions reducing cost-of-living benefits, a threatened increase in faculty workload, and in the anticipation of collective-bargaining legislation in the state of California. While not yet a dominant political force in the life of the campus, such organizations may be regarded as a direct political response to the budgetary exigencies mentioned, and stand as potentially major political groups in the determination of personnel policies in the University.

The Bureaucratic Dimension: the Proliferation of Procedures

Administrative arrangements in universities have also undergone a process of elaboration during the past two decades. In making this point, we are not maintaining necessarily that there has been an increased reliance on power and authority—at the expense, for example, of collegial influence—in institutions of higher learning. We know of no way of assessing such a development empirically. We can be more nearly certain, however, of the development of a range of new procedures, and a corresponding formalization of academic life. Part of this is an inherited consequence of the rapid period of growth in the 1950s and 1960s. As individual campuses increased in size, and in numbers of academic programs and organized research activities, the requirements for administrative coordination and management increased correspondingly. As individual campuses were linked to state-wide or system-wide systems of campuses, moreover, that development likewise produced an impetus to create system-wide procedures and mechanisms of coordination.

We point also to a less conspicuous source of bureaucratic proliferation: the tendency on the part of organizations, under conditions of uncertainty and political conflict, to develop rules and procedures which not only serve as guides to policy and action but also reduce the organization's vulnerability to criticism on the part of interested political constituencies. We give three instances of this in Berkeley's recent administrative history, the last of which deals directly with academic recruitment.

The first example concerns faculty teaching. One of the persistent criticisms voiced repeatedly in the past two decades—though such criticisms are not entirely new—is that the faculty role unduly emphasizes scientific and scholarly research, and that its teaching responsibilities to students have been correspondingly slighted. Such criticism appeared in the protests of various student activist groups in the 1960s; it remains a preoccupation of organizations like the study lobby; and it has found expression on the part of economy-minded legislators and state executives who argue that the faculty's primary mission is teaching, not research and related activities. Setting aside the issue of whether such assertions are justified, we may note that the atmosphere of continued political criticism has generated a number of new activities and procedures at various places in the university. At the system-wide administrative level, there have been developed a number of efforts to measure time spent in teaching, some of which involve rather elaborate responses to questionnaires, timekeeping of the faculty's daily activities, and the like. At the campus level, some academic departments have instituted systems of student evaluation of courses. The campus administration has established an office to assist departments in that activity, and chairpersons are now required to provide quantitative documentation of teaching ability—usually in the form of results of student surveys—for all cases of advancement or promotion of a faculty member. Such procedures serve to increase information on teaching activities, to convert that information-gathering activity into an everyday bureaucratic routine, and to provide the campus with evidence that it is taking the teaching activities of its faculty seriously, thus tending to blunt criticisms that it is not.

The second example concerns faculty conduct. During the last major episode of political turmoil on the Berkeley campus in the spring of 1970—the protest against the military incursion into Cambodia by the Nixon administration—one major form that political activity took was to attempt to "reconstitute" academic classes into political discussion and action groups. Over a period of two months a number of classes were canceled, and many took a form conspicuously different from that originally advertised in course descriptions. Heated criticisms of "irresponsible" faculty members were heard during the episode and for months afterward. The subsequent decision of the California legislature to deny a cost-of-living salary increase was widely regarded as a punitive measure against the faculty. Criticism continued, and the system-wide administration took measures to prepare some kind of "faculty code of conduct" that would specify classroom and related responsibilities of faculty members. Under that pressure, the Academic Senate of the University itself produced a code which, after a period of negotiation with the administration, was adopted as a series of guidelines for class content, class scheduling, class disruption, and related matters. Since that document envisioned the possibility of disciplining faculty members, it also included a number of procedures for "due process" in the event of such action. The faculty code of conduct has not proved to be a very important document since its enactment, but it still stands as an example of responding to uncertainty and conflict by preparing a set of rules and instituting a series of procedures for their enforcement.

The third example, closer to home, concerns affirmative action in academic recruitment. Whereas much of the discussion of affirmative-action programs in the late 1960s and early 1970s involved an explicit discussion of distinct "goals" or "targets" for future recruitment of minorities and women in faculty positions, the actual implementation of the affirmative-action impulse took the form of establishing certain procedures that all recruiting units were to follow. These included insuring that the position was adequately publicized, that minority groups and women received certain preferential treatment (for example, by earmarking certain funds to them for traveling for interviews), and that, above all, the recruiting unit provide an elaborate report and justification of how it organized the search, how it evaluated the candidates who applied, and on what basis it made decisions among finalist candidates. Our survey of several comparison institutions indicates that the development of such procedures is a fairly typical response to affirmative-action pressures. Certainly these procedures defined the conditions of our search and constituted one of its most time-consuming features. We shall comment on their usefulness presently.

Such are the major contours of institutional change in the past two decades for higher education: a dramatic cycle of rapid growth followed by slow growth, transforming the market for academic services from a seller's into a buyer's market; a parade of political disturbances and developments that has rendered the political dimension of academic life more salient and more complex; and—arising from this complicated pattern of growth, stagnation, and conflict—a tendency to "proceduralize" an ever-wider range of academic activities, thus developing the bureaucratic component of university life. We cannot claim that these changes are completely general, for we have relied on evidence from a limited range of institutions. Furthermore, only some of the changes we have characterized bear on the recruitment process itself, and only some of those directly so. Nevertheless, we feel confident in asserting that these economic, political, and administrative changes constitute the major lines of deviation from the Caplow and McGee model, and that there has been a decline in importance of the mechanism of collegial influence and consensus as the basis for academic recruitment.

Microscopic Implications of the Changes

Taken together, the several institutional changes we have just traced boil down to a single, paradoxical demand on recruiting academic units: while these units are under pressure to recruit fewer new faculty members, they are simultaneously being asked to devote more time and resources to the recruitment process. The limited availability of new positions, combined with the continuing appearance of new Ph.D.'s on the market, means that there will be more applications for each position, thus increasing the amount of processing required of the hiring units. Values of equity, moreover, call for fairness and thoroughness in treating each application, which also calls for increased time and energy. In the interests of affirmative action, academic units are being required to make their recruitment increasingly public through advertising an open search, which also tends to increase the number of applicants. Finally—and also connected with affirmative action—there is the expectation that extra efforts should be made to seek out and give consideration to previously disadvantaged candidates, and that those efforts should be reported in detail. The paradox emerges when, in conjunction with these demands to expend greater resources, the wherewithal to develop those resources in the tangible form of increased departmental budgets is not forthcoming. Indeed, the tendency has been to reduce departmental budgets and to press, not always successfully, for increasing the competing uses of faculty and administrative departmental resources.

The foregoing account also reveals that the decision-making context for academic administrators has grown more complicated. Within the collegial network model described by Caplow and McGee, the main political problem is gaining consensus among colleagues. Within the model of the "fiduciary collegial association" advanced by Parsons and Platt, the main political problem is legitimizing decisions by referring them to the appropriate cognitive or disciplinary standards. Such a judgment is oversimple, for both the Caplow-McGee and Parsons-Platt analyses take into account conflicts between colleagues and the often precarious character of collegial consensus. Notwithstanding, we would suggest that in the past two decades a number of new conflicting if not contradictory forces have been superimposed on the values of excellence and collegial consensus. In recruiting, academic decision-makers are still under pressure—much of it internalized as their own personal values—to sustain and continue to develop the traditions of scientific and scholarly excellence rooted in the academy. But at the same time they are deprived of resources to implement those diverse goals. They are under pressure to reach "targets" for affirmative action, but find difficulty in reaching *any* kind of target because of the diminished resources and lack of new positions. And although the values of scientific and scholarly excellence and the goals of affirmative action may not be conflicting in principle, they appear to be so in the minds of many, and hence constitute the basis for conflict and polarization. The same administrators are asked to be more equitable, thorough, and exhaustive in evaluating their vastly increased numbers of potential recruits, but to do so with diminishing resources. In short, the current confluence of cultural, political, and economic forces that have converged on the academy has altered the terms of academic leadership. The charge facing that leadership has moved a degree farther *away* from an ideal situation in which leaders are asked to engineer consensus within a context of striving for excellence, and a degree *closer to* a situation in which leaders must mediate between an increased number of constituencies both within and outside the academic department, constituencies that press a number of conflicting criteria for decision-making. In such a context, successful leadership calls more for strategies of navigation among conflicting goals than for strategies of maximization of a single set of goals.

THE BERKELEY CASE STUDY IN THE FOREGOING CONTEXT

Our own search took place in the context of the kind of environment we have described in this chapter. The Berkeley Sociology Department had enjoyed a season of growth for a period of approximately one and one-half decades, leveling off to a "no-growth" plateau during the five or so years preceding 1975–76. We were committed to the values of excellence in science and scholarship (though the Department was divided on exactly what those values meant and how they ought to be implemented). As buyers, we were aware that we were in an advantageous position in the sense of having a superabundance of talent to consider among our applicants; we were also aware, however, that we might not have our absolute pick, since competition between Berkeley and a number of other leading universities was likely to be brisk. Moreover, in seeking out and considering applicants, we were attentive to publicizing the positions widely, giving each as thorough and as fair an evaluation as possible, reporting on our procedures, and giving special attention to the sex and ethnic characteristics of the pool of applicants. The one exception to the general market picture was that we had, for that brief period, a relative abundance of positions to fill. At the same time, however, we did not have a particular abundance of resources available to carry out the search.

Examining our effort in retrospect, we conclude that our diverse efforts seemed to boil down to a single general strategy: to expand and reorganize our resources in order to meet the various exigencies we faced in carrying out the search in the existing environment. We expanded faculty participation, by altering the committee structure and more than doubling the number of committee members, and by urging the remainder of the faculty to participate by reading candidates' materials, by coming and listening critically to their presentations, and by interviewing them. By reorganizing the non-academic staff, we more than tripled (at least by our estimation) the amount of such staff support from previous years. By securing the computer terminal and the magnetic-card typewriter, we greatly augmented our capacity to process and store the mountains of information that necessarily accumulated, given the scope of the operation. And finally, we expanded the input of administrative time, mostly our own, by "keeping on top" of the flow of the process, persuading colleagues to complete their work, and attempting to influence—insofar as that was possible—the political process that unfolded as we moved to a departmental decision on which of the candidates to interview and ultimately to hire. To support that expansion and reorganization of resources, we relied on specially augmented financial contributions (which we secured by aggressive, piecemeal begging from campus administrative offices), on authority (exercised in reallocating non-academic personnel), and on influence (exercised mainly in the form of persuading faculty members and to a lesser extent graduate students to participate responsibly in the recruitment process). This conclusion is not especially startling or dramatic, but it strikes us as correct. Furthermore, we believe that expanding and reorganizing resources were practically the only adaptations available to us, given the peculiar combination of constraints and exigencies we faced.

We might ask of this search: in what respects was it a success and in what respects a failure?

It was a success in the sense that it did not grind to a halt by failure of the involved Department participants to complete the necessary work in the necessary time, and in the sense that it was not paralyzed by political conflict among faculty members in the Department. This may not appear to be much of a success at first glance. Those of us involved, however, were always fully aware of the continuous threats to the successful continuation of the search. We have since become aware, from interviews with campus administrators and colleagues in other departments around the country, that a very high proportion of new positions go unfilled every year through departmental inability to keep a search going.

It was a success in the sense that we were able to give equally thorough consideration to each candidate who applied.

It was a success in the most obvious sense of the term; we were able to interview every candidate we chose to interview, and we were successful in hiring every candidate to whom we extended an offer, even though all had several alternative positions available.

It was a success in the sense that we lived up to the *currently existing* requirements for affirmative action—casting a wide net, reducing arbitrariness in the evaluation of any candidates, recording and reporting on the sex and ethnic composition of our pool of candidates, and on the reasons for our ultimate decisions.

It was an unanticipated success in that in our effort to maximize thoroughness and objectivity, we involved a great many faculty members from the beginning; this appeared to give credibility to the process and lessened the probability of any of the recommendations being blocked by opposing faculty groups.

It was a failure, we believe, in terms of the effectiveness with which we communicated with the unsuccessful candidates. We were conscientious in answering queries and other correspondence, in attempting to gather materials from candidates, and in informing them in as diplomatic a way as possible after we had decided they were no longer in the competition. Yet, caught up mostly in our own efforts to keep the process moving more or less as we had planned it, we failed to communicate to almost all of the candidates what our own processes were and why we were doing what we were doing. We noted in many instances that high expectations were generated when the realistic chances of ultimate appointment were virtually nil. We observed anxiety and irritation on the part of numerous candidates and their sponsors. Perhaps these reactions are inevitable in a large, public search. Nevertheless, we remain dissatisfied with the way in which we communicated with the candidates.

Finally, the search was a failure in the sense that so much of our work seemed to be wasted. Though we advertised widely and we encouraged the application of minorities and women, the final result of the search—in terms of persons invited for interviews and in terms of persons actually appointed—was much the same as it would have been if we had simply written letters to colleagues in the dozen leading departments and asked them to name their best students.[9] We were aware of this at the

9. The one exception to this was the appearance of the two candidates who were ultimately appointed whom we contacted through the annual meetings of the American Sociological Association; but one of these turned up through another source later, and we do not know whether the other one would have done so as well.

time of the search. Toward the end, when we knew generally who the successful candidates were going to be, we developed a somewhat bitter joke that the whole thing could have been done for the cost of two 13-cent stamps to send letters to a colleague at Chicago and a colleague at Harvard. We satisfied our consciences by the public advertising and the thoroughness of the review; we satisfied the requirements laid down by university administrators that the advertisement be placed and the reports be filed; they in turn satisfied others looking over their shoulders. Yet the *effective* result of that process was mainly a tremendous increase in the amount of paperwork—both in files to be read and reports to be filed. The "new" market thus appears to be characterized mainly by increased costs in faculty time, departmental resources, and candidate anxieties, but not, from all we could observe, by different results in recruitment patterns.

This last set of observations is sobering, and leads us to some further reflections. Earlier we noted that the recruitment process could be regarded as a succesion of decisions to *exclude* candidates from the potential pool, whether these decisions are made by the candidate (who may not bother to apply, thus taking himself out of the running) or by those who are evaluating the candidate according to various criteria. Among these exclusionary criteria, we mentioned specifying the position so as to exclude some types of candidates (for example, non-demographers if the position calls for someone with demographic skills), judging the candidates according to standards of achievement and promise, relying on known and trusted recommendations by colleagues, and taking into account past or present discrimination. There is no automatic application of any of these criteria at any given stage of the recruitment process, but the cumulative effect is a remarkable telescoping toward a few candidates from a few leading institutions; as such, the entire process appears to have an overdetermined if not a predestined outcome. Consider the following processes of narrowing:

1. By the time we initiated our search, the potential pool of applicants was *already* narrowed extremely from all possible candidates in the relevant age-cohort (say, from 25 to 40 years of age). This narrowing had occurred at all stages of the socialization and education process, cutting off from consideration, at various stages, those who did not finish high school; those who finished high school but did not attend college; those who did attend college but did not finish; and those who finished college who did not go on to advanced professional training in sociology or a closely allied social science. In our job description, we narrowed the field further by insisting that the candidate be finished or almost finished with the Ph.D., and that he or she fall into one or another of three broadly-defined subfields of sociology.

2. The distribution of the institutional origins of our pool of candidates, when compared with the generality of Ph.D.s in that general age cohort, suggests that a certain amount of self-selection occurs in response to a publicly advertised position by a distinguished department in a distinguished university.

3. On the basis of our interviews with representatives of some other institutions and the basis of our own experience in placing advanced graduate students, there is also evidence of a certain selection among students *within* a Ph.D.-attaining cohort, with the "best" of those students being recommended or encouraged to apply to the "best" departments and institutions, while others are discouraged from doing so.

4. A further skewing occurred in our preliminary evaluation when we decided which candidates were to be interviewed and, beyond those, which candidates were "strong" and "not strong." We judged as "not strong" 75 percent of those from the top-ranking half-dozen sociology departments; 83 percent received this judgment from the next-ranking list of departments, and 80 percent from the

third-ranking list. From the lowest-ranking set of departments, fully 98 percent of the applicants were judged to be "not strong." By this time the competition was mainly among candidates from the two top-ranked categories of sociology departments, with only 6 out of 35 "strong" or "interviewed" candidates coming from the lower two ranks of departments (see Table 3, Chapter Seven).

5. Turning to a finer discrimination between our 35 candidates who were "hired and/or interviewed" and those who were "not interviewed but strong," even more candidates from the lower-ranking institutions were excluded. We reproduce here a portion of Table 3, from Chapter Seven, to show that result:

TABLE A
Quality of Institution of Candidate

Final Evaluation of Berkeley candidate	N	*I%*	N	*II%*	N	*III%*	N	*IV%*	N	*Total%*
Hired and/or interviewed	8	44	3	27	0	0	0	0	11	31
Not interviewed but strong	10	56	8	73	5	100	1	100	24	69
Totals	18	100	11	100	5	100	1	100	35	100

By this stage all candidates from the lower two prestige ranks of departments had been excluded, and among those that were to be "interviewed"—that is, those with a realistic "shot" at the position, almost three-quarters were from the first prestige rank of departments.

6. Finally, the distinction between those who were ultimately hired and those who were "interviewed but not hired" presses the narrowing process virtually to its ultimate end:

TABLE B
Quality of Institution of Candidate

Final Evaluation of Berkeley Candidate	N	I%	N	II%	N	III%	N	IV%	N	Total%
Hired	3	60	1	33	0	—	0	—	4	36
Interviewed but not hired	5	40	2	67	0	—	0	—	7	64
Totals	8	100	3	100	0	—	0	—	11	100

The telescoping process is consistent and extreme, and reflects the lifetime cumulation of the forces of differential socialization and differential opportunity, self-selection, and the progressive accumulation of advantage through training at institutions of high academic prestige and quality.

These data and observations lead to one final reflection. Since the telescoping forces are so dominant even before candidates enter the academic market, we would question the potential of somewhat "mechanical" requirements (such as public advertisements and submitting written reports) for changing the fundamental process that is at work. At Berkeley in 1975–76 we did a great deal to assure that not only outstanding, mostly white, mostly male students from leading institutions would be considered for our positions. We know of no other case that approached the thoroughness of our search and review process. But unless we had actively discriminated against leading institutions or certain ethnic or sex groupings, the result was—and, we believe, would again be—virtually the same as if the entire process had never been undertaken. In many respects, the careers of individuals are "too far along"—in the sense of having been predetermined by earlier processes of socialization and selection—for us to expect that the outcome would be otherwise. Despite the many changes in the academic market that we have noted in our account, it remains the case that the leading institutions continue to generate "short lists" of leading candidates from other leading institutions, which are very similar in composition. The main question then becomes, which of the leading institutions will get which of the few? This is an undramatic and somewhat pessimistic conclusion for those of us who have put so much thought and work into the business of searching in the market, but all the facts we have observed and all the impressions we have gained lead to no other.

A FEW RECOMMENDATIONS

Under this heading we may be brief, since what we have to say has been implicit in many of the conclusions we have already drawn in this chapter. Nevertheless, we can say a few explicit words under three headings.

The Supply of New Ph.D.'s

Throughout, we have observed that the decisions on the part of faculty and administrators affecting the level of training in various academic disciplines are somewhat insulated from market conditions and rooted in other considerations. Among these considerations are the department's or the university's place in the general prestige hierarchy, and the degree to which it believes the aggressive development of graduate-training and research centers will move it upward in that hierarchy; the generosity of boards of trustees or state legislatures; the entrepreneurial and persuasive skills of department chairpersons; and the like. The result of this situation is that, when economic conditions do call for a constriction of supply, there are very few automatic "brakes" in the system that will make for the necessary constriction.

Our recommendation would be, simply, that efforts be made to improve the knowledge of future trends in demand and supply, and that responsible organizations develop mechanisms so that these trends can be taken into account in setting admissions policies. Certainly the appropriate professional associations can place high priority on generating better information about market conditions, as can appropriate government agencies, such as the National Academy of Science. Various groups, such as department chairpersons who meet annually at many of the professional associations' conventions, or the American Association of Graduate Deans, could take steps toward combating the decentralized, "free-for-all" pattern of contemporary decision-making, and toward coordinating their policy recommendations with respect to admissions and anticipated production of Ph.D.'s. This recommendation, while not completely specific in form, nonetheless appears to be the most important one we could venture, since oversupply is and promises to continue to be the source of so many of the difficulties in the market for academic services.

Recruitment

Insofar as the currently institutionalized procedures that define "affirmative action" continue to exist and to enjoy legitimacy—procedures such as public advertising, undertaking specific efforts to uncover talented minority and women candidates, and filing extensive reports on the results of public searches—we see no other alternative than to increase the resources devoted to academic searches. To make them as thorough, effective, and fair as possible, it is necessary to increase faculty involvement, non-academic staff involvement, and technological supports.

The easiest and most respectable recommendation to make with respect to affirmative action would be to scold ourselves and others for not being dedicated and thorough enough, and call for more and more aggressive efforts to locate talented individuals from groups that have been underrepresented in the academy. Quite obviously, we do not recommend any *less* effort of that sort, and we would urge those who conduct closed, casual searches over a limited field of candidates to open and systematize them. Yet our analysis has led us to wonder whether the directions that affirmative-action measures have taken up to this point have been the most fruitful directions, and whether redoubling the kinds of efforts made in the past is the wisest course. We did something of that sort in our own search, and ended up concluding that such efforts made little difference in the ultimate outcome. We believe that if we had done more—such as direct advertising and encouragement specifically to certain groups, and telephoning faculty members around the country who were likely to have talented students in training—we might have altered somewhat the composition of our ultimate pool of candidates, but the telescoped outcome we described would not have been altered.

Would not wisdom dictate that, rather than throwing more and more time and energy into procedures that are simultaneously draining on resources and questionably effective, the effort on the part of academics along affirmative-action lines be more diversified? We do not advocate a return to "closed" recruiting; certainly positions should continue to be advertised and searches should attempt to locate talented young professionals who might self-select themselves out or otherwise remain invisible. Given limited resources, however, it seems to us that more attention should be given to nurturing that talent through programs of admission, through active efforts to locate promising and intelligent minority and women students at the undergraduate level, to interest them in the field, and to develop commitments and skills that will point them toward advanced graduate work and professional academic careers. To recommend this is not to shun responsibility at the level of recruitment; it is rather to call for a more effective redirection of resources toward the same goals.

The final recommendation we have in the area of recruitment is that the faculties and administrations of recruiting institutions apprise themselves of the human costs—mainly to candidates—that are involved in large public searches and make every effort to take the sensitivities of the candidates into account, even though it is "in the cards" that virtually all of them will end up as losers in the competition.

Placement

One of the ways that candidates' sensitivities can be taken into account is to improve communication with those who apply. Another more direct but perhaps more important way is for graduate academic departments to develop much more systematic efforts to cooperate with their *own* students who are seeking placement in other institutions. As we saw in Chapter Three, efforts to systematize placement have been relatively minor in the sample of institutions we visited. We believe that faculties of departments could improve the lives of their students if they would take measures such as the following:

1. Develop a placement committee of at least two faculty members, one senior and one who has recently been on the job market, to advise and assist graduate students.

2. Advise students early—perhaps as much as six months before they go on the market—about customs of applying for positions and preparing curricula vitae. Graduate students recently in the market could share their experiences with those about to go forward.

3. Have the placement committee talk individually with students and their main faculty sponsors about the students' interests, ambitions, and competences.

4. Meet collectively with students "on the market" periodically during the season of recruitment, so that information, impressions, and experience can be shared.

5. Institute presentations, mock interviews, and the like with faculty and graduate students at the home institution.

6. Inform the students of the home institution's goals and procedures in recruiting.

Such practices are of limited utility, of course, because they do not strike at the causes of the problems that plague the market at this time in its history. Nevertheless, they would be helpful in providing information to, reducing the anxieties of, and improving the strategies of candidates in that market, most of whom now find themselves in a sea of mystery and uncertainty.

A CONCLUDING WORD

This concludes our account and our interpretations of it. We have attempted to move back and forth from an analysis of the most general economic, political, social, and cultural forces that have come to bear on the market for those with advanced academic training, to the most specific challenges that these forces generate in a single search in a single department. The latter aspect of our account has the limitations of any case study. Its findings cannot be generalized to all other searches and all other departments, whose own histories and own contemporary situations differ from our own. We are convinced, however, that the larger forces impinging on the entire market for academic services are sufficiently similar and pervasive that most institutions of higher education are struggling with the same issues and dilemmas that preoccupied us. For this reason, the experiences of one may be instructive for the many.

ASA *Footnotes*

University of California, Berkeley. The Department of Sociology anticipates that three Assistant Professor positions will be open, beginning Fall Quarter, 1976. The Department intends to appoint the most highly qualified candidates in the following fields: (1) quantitative research methods, but without specification with respect to substantive area. (2) comparative studies. The Department is especially interested in those who have background in comparative research relating to China, Africa, or Latin America. (3) demography, stratification, or urban sociology, or some combination of these related sub-fields. Minorities and women are encouraged to apply. Applicants should write, enclosing resume, to: Chair, Box F, Department of Sociology, University of California, Berkeley, CA 94720.

Guidelines for Evaluating Candidates

TO: Members of the Personnel Committee and Subcommittees

FROM: Neil J. Smelser, Chairman

As you know, the Personnel Committee has agreed upon an evaluation procedure for candidates applying for the faculty positions that we anticipate for 1975–76. Each candidate will be evaluated on three criteria: (1) career pattern to date; (2) written work; (3) letters of recommendation. An evaluation sheet (see attached sample) will be provided each reviewer, who will be asked to assign a score of 1–5 on each criterion, and to jot down any additional impressions he or she may have of the candidate.

The purpose of this memo is to provide a suggested list of more specific guidelines, or questions that might be asked under each general criterion.

CAREER PATTERN TO DATE

1. What is the quality of the institutions in which the individual received his/her undergraduate and graduate education?

2. What kinds of awards or other acknowledgments of academic achievement has the candidate received (Phi Beta Kappa, departmental citations, marks of "distinction" on examinations, competitive scholarships, post-doctoral fellowships, etc.)?

3. In what kinds of research has the candidate participated, and in what capacities (e.g., research assistant)? Is there any evidence on the quality of that research experience?

4. What kind of teaching experience has the candidate had as a student (e.g., teaching assistant, part-time instructor)? Is there any evidence on the quality of that teaching?

5. What kind of post-educational teaching experience has the candidate had? In what quality of institution? Is there any evidence on the quality of that teaching?

6. Has the candidate acquired or had any experiences that are not specifically "sociological" in character but which should be noted as relevant to a sociological career (e.g., knowledge of one or more foreign languages, a period of residence in a developing country, employment as a secretary, reporter, dishwasher, etc.)?

7. Is the candidate qualified in any academic fields other than sociology (e.g., history, mathematics, linguistics)?

8. Is there evidence of post-educational professional recognition (e.g., service as a referee on a scholarly journal, prizes for publications, etc.)?

WRITTEN WORK

1. Is the work novel or creative with respect to the formulation of a problem, the execution of research, or the theoretical interpretation of results?

2. If the research involves empirical investigation, how adequate is its design? Are the research methods appropriate to the problem under investigation? Are the data that have been analyzed the most appropriate data?

3. Does the candidate show a particular theoretical flair with respect to formal theory construction, codification or synthesis of ideas, or especially penetrating insights into or criticisms of others' theoretical formulations?

4. How adequate or excellent is the candidate's style of writing?

5. Is the candidate especially productive or unproductive with regard to the quantity of written work?

6. In what kinds of publication, if any, has the candidate's written work resulted? Competitive, prestige, main-line journals? Specialized journals? Non-sociological journals? Magazines?

LETTERS OF RECOMMENDATION

1. What is the manifest tone of the letters of recommendation? Chilly? Lukewarm? Positive? Raving?

2. In what capacity, and how well does the referee appear to know the candidate?

3. Are the letters general or specific, vague or precise, with respect to the candidate's qualities?

4. What strengths and weaknesses are stressed by the referee?

5. Does the referee appear unequivocal in his/her message, or does there seem to be an additional message between the lines?

6. What is the reputation of the referee in terms of his/her institutional identification? In terms of his/her excellence as a scholar and teacher? In terms of his/her credibility?

7. Does the referee explicitiy compare the candidate with other past or present candidates? If not, are other letters on other candidates available, so that such comparisons can be inferred?

APPENDIX C

Personnel Committee
Faculty Evaluation Form

NOTE TO EVALUATORS: *Please,* commit yourself to one of
the five categories and *do not* add intermediate points on the
scale. Please review the guidelines for evaluators prepared by
Neil J. Smelser before completing this form. Additionally,
please make appropriate notes as to the reasons for your evaluation (especially with respect to cases which seem particularly
strong in any respect). Comments may be continued on the back
of this sheet if necessary.

CANDIDATE _____

EVALUATOR _____ DATE ____

Ranking of the Candidate's potential for a faculty position at
Berkeley as demonstrated by:

A. CAREER TO DATE:

_____ 1. Excellent COMMENTS: (continue on back if necessary)

_____ 2. Good

_____ 3. Average

_____ 4. Below Average

_____ 5. Poor

B. QUALITY OF WRITTEN WORK

_____ 1. Excellent COMMENTS: (continue on back if necessary)

_____ 2. Good

_____ 3. Average

_____ 4. Below Average

_____ 5. Poor

C. LETTERS OF RECOMMENDATION

_____ 1. Excellent COMMENTS: (continue on back if necessary)

_____ 2. Good

_____ 3. Average

_____ 4. Below Average

_____ 5. Poor

Candidate Information Form

Name:

Address:

Phone Number:

Gender:

Ethnicity:

Fields of Specialization in Order of Importance (See attached list for standardized field designations):

1. _____

2. _____

3. _____

Index

Academic market: defined, 2–3; buyers and sellers, 2–3; relation to non-academic positions, 3–4, 48–49; traditional criteria, 4–5; comparison to economic model, 9, 158–159; lack of information within, 12–13; labor supply, 31–32, 33; response to fluctuations, 32–33, 34; supply and demand, 36–39; relation to affirmative action, 41–42; effect of change on sociology departments, 43; response of students to declining demand, 49, 111–112. *See also* Higher education institutions; Placement; Recruitment

The Academic Marketplace, 13–14. *See also* Caplow, Theodore and Reece McGee

Affirmative action: basis for, 24; criteria within, 25–26; conflict with universal criteria, 29–30; relation to changes in academic market, 41–42; goals and means, 54–55, 56, 169–170; at Indiana University, 55–56; at University of California, effects on sociology department, 68–69; at University of California, faculty attitudes, 69, 84–85; at University of California, conflict over incident, 69–70; procedural requirements, 73–74, 145–146; information requested of candidates, 110, 111, 191; response to questionnaire by white males, 111, 147; role in joint appointment, 132; effectiveness, 181–182; recommendations, 182–183; questionnaire, 191. *See also* Candidates; Minorities and women; Search

American Council on Education, 38, 45, 66, 139–140. *See also* Cartter, Allan M.

American Federation of Teachers, 166

American Sociological Association: placement bureau, 17–18, 55, 88, 101–104, 144; Executive Office placement survey, 38–39; affirmative action policies, 40; *Footnotes,* 40, 58, 74, 88, 89, 144; employment bulletin, 55, 58; response to tightening academic market, 56–58; Committee on Expanding Employment Opportunities for Sociologists, 57, 58; Executive Associate for Careers, Minorities, and Women, 57, 58, 59; role in placement process, 59–60; investigation of Berkeley hiring

Institutions, 63–65; growth of,
64–65; size in 1966, 67; role of
Frederick Teggart, 63; divisions
within, contributing factors,
66–67, 80–81, 81–85;
affirmative action pressures on,
68–69; conflicts on affirmative
action within, 69–70;
recruitment patterns, 1952–1964,
65–66; recruitment changes after
1966, 67–68; recruitment
procedures, 1952–1975, 70–72;
role of chairman, 70–72 (*See also*
Smelser, Neil J.); personnel
committee, 70–71, 74–76, 115;
personnel committee,
reorganization of, 91–93;
personnel committee evaluation
form, 189–190; changes in
faculty makeup, 67–68, 73,
74–75; faculty vacancies, 74–76,
78–80 (*See also* Comparative
Methods position; Demography
and Urban Stratification position;
Quantitative Methods position);
recruitment failure, 1974–75,
74–76; five-year plan, 78–79;
factions within, 84–85,
124–125, 126–127; need for
consensus on appointees, 90–91;
division over candidates, 122,
124–126; joint appointment,
132. *See also* Search
Discrimination, 23–24, 29. *See also*
Affirmative action; Minorities and
women

Economic model. *See* Academic
market; Higher education
institutions
Exclusion: in recruitment process,
26–29; by social factors,
177–178. *See also* Review

Faculty: number tenured, 36;
workload of placement, 49,
183–184; workload of

recruitment, 50, 72, 182–183;
attitudes toward specialization,
81; participation in review
process, 105; reactions to
computer, 108–109; demands of
buyers' market, 111–112;
participation in candidates' visits,
117–118; organizations, 166;
student criticism of, 167–168;
conduct, 168–169. *See also*
Department; Higher education
institutions
Ferriss, Abbott L., 37
Finsterbusch, Kurt, 38
Footnotes. See American Sociological
Association
Free Speech Movement, 66

Graduate students: role in search
process, 51, 95–96; faculty
attitudes toward, 84; positions
toward finalists, 125, 126. *See
also* Higher education institutions

Higher education institutions:
expansion of, 14, 35; financial
support, 34, 40; teacher shortage,
35–36; number of doctorates, 36;
political pressures on, 39–40; role
in rising expectations, 41; analysis
by Caplow and McGee, 156–157,
159; analysis by Parsons and
Platt, 157–159; economic model,
159, 162–164; bureaucratic
model, 159–160; democratic
association model, 159, 160;
stresses of reduced demand,
162–164; political challenges,
164–167; growth of bureaucracy,
167–170; conflicting demands
on, 170–172

Indiana University, affirmative
action procedures, 55–56
Influence networks, 13–14, 17, 23,
72, 101, 135; relation to
information, 17; in non-academic

plan for, 88–99; technological aids, 86, 96–98, 107–109, 113; sources, 88–90; graduate student involvement, 95; within same institution, 119–120; sources, relative to candidates' institutional ranking, 143; sources, relative to candidates' ranking, 144–145; reasons for narrow base, 176–180. *See also* Search

Review: by non-academic staff, 51; streamlining process, 52–53; workload of, 53–54, 72; visit and interview, 53–54; technological aids, 96–98, 107–109, 113; by committees, 93–94; evaluation structure, 94–95; factors in evaluation, 142; evaluation guidelines, 186–188

Salary, 4, 6–7; relation to prestige, 19; as fixed cost, 36

Search: failure of (1975), 74–76; demands on resources, 76, 85–86, 105–107; goals, 87–88; role of committees, 91–93; role of non-academic staff, 96; subcommittee procedures, 112–113, 115; technical aids, funding for, 105–106; advertising, 88–89, 185; number of applicants, 100, 132; lack of application deadline, 104–105; pressure of time, 106, 116, 120–121, 123–124; consensus on active candidates, 113–115; visits, 115–116; importance of visits, 116–117; problems of visits, 117; brutalizing aspects, 116, 118, 133–134; evaluation of, 174–176. *See also* Department; Recruitment; Smelser, Neil J.

Self-selection, 28–29, 103; by minorities, 148

Smelser, Neil J.: visit to ASA office, 45; actions during recruitment

failure (1974–75), 74–76; preparation of five-year plan, 78, 79; role in rational recruitment plan, 86, 88, 89, 90, 91, 94, 96; interviews at placement bureau, 103; computer incident, 107; in review process, 115, 117; feelings toward candidates, 118; view of possible conflicts, 121, 123, 124, 125, 126; support of Candidate X, 126; role in Departmental decisions, 128, 129; dealings with successful candidates, 130–131

Sociology: theoretical schools within, 11–12; founders, 62; sub-fields, relative to minorities and women, 29; sub-fields, vacancies in, 78–80; supply and demand within, 37–39; enrollment policy response to market, 46; placement, response to market, 46–49; academic view of non-academic positions, 48–49; role of non-academic sociologists within, 57. *See also* Department

Stratification, in higher education institutions, 158–160

Strong, Edward H., 64, 65

Technology, use in recruitment, 86, 96–98, 107–109, 113

Teggart, Frederick, 63

Tenure, 9–10, 34, 36, 163; denials of, 46

Universities: ranking, 6–7, 38, 45, 66, 139; comparable to Berkeley, 43–45. *See also* Higher education institutions

University of California, Berkeley: College of Letters and Science, 78, 85–86; administration approval for search, 77, 79;

Compositor: Lienett Company, Inc.
Printer: Thomson-Shore, Inc.
Binder: John Dekker and Sons
Text: VIP Garamond
Display: VIP Garamond
Cloth: Holliston Roxite A 50234
Paper: 50 lb P&S offset vellum